1968: The Election
That Changed America

1968:
THE ELECTION
THAT CHANGED
AMERICA

Lewis L. Gould

Second Edition

The American Ways Series

IVAN R. DEE *Chicago*

www.ivanrdee.com

Library of Congress Cataloging-in-Publication Data:
Gould, Lewis L.
    1968 : the election that changed America / Lewis L. Gould. — 2nd ed.
[eagle logo].
        p. cm. — (The american ways series)
    Includes bibliographical references and index.
    ISBN 978-1-56663-862-3 (pbk. : alk. paper)
    1. Presidents—United States—Election—1968. 2. Elections—
United States—History—20th century. 3. United States—Politics and
government—1963–1969. I. Title.
JK1968 1968
324.973'0923—dc22   2009049669

Contents

initiative. Nixon and South Vietnam. The Humphrey surge and Nixon's response. The election results and their meaning.

Preface to the First Edition

BY THE 1990s public disenchantment with politics in the United States had reached intense levels. Huge budget deficits, a persistent economic slowdown, and unmet social problems focused popular unhappiness on the political system and its flaws. A generation of divided government, in which Republicans dominated the presidency while Democrats controlled Congress, had produced an apparent gridlock in Washington which stalled constructive responses to the nation's needs. Angry voters flirted with third parties or grew apathetic toward politics altogether.

The origins of these problems extended back into the mid-1960s when the Democratic party waged an unpopular war in Vietnam, pursued a Great Society in domestic affairs, and dealt with long-deferred issues of civil rights for black citizens. By 1968, however, the war in Vietnam had become stalemated. Liberal programs to improve the lives of the poor and minorities provoked bitter opposition among white Americans. As a result, the presidential election of 1968 became a contest in which the passions and violence of the society surged into the political arena. Assassinations, urban rioting, and war added new volatility to national politics.

The outcome of the election left no one fully satisfied. The Republicans put Richard Nixon in the White House, but the Democrats retained control of both houses of Congress. Radicals were frustrated that the nation had not embraced social revolution. Conservatives resented the residual strength of liberal ideas. The issue of race had not been addressed nor its effects diminished. A close election had left things much as they had been when the year began—or so it seemed on the surface.

In fact the 1968 election proved to be a watershed event in American politics. Republicans used the skills they brought to Nixon's campaign to create an ascendancy in presidential politics. Democrats, divided and torn after 1968, emerged as only crippled challengers for the White House in the 1970s and 1980s. Bitterness over racial issues and discord on the Vietnam War continued to shape national affairs. The events of 1968 changed the way Americans felt about politics and their leaders. An erosion of confidence in American institutions began that has not yet reached a conclusion.

Soon after Nixon took office, books appeared to explain the trauma through which the country had passed. Since those early accounts, historians and journalists have reexamined 1968, most often in the context of the rebellious college students who rallied to liberal Democrats such as Eugene McCarthy and Robert F. Kennedy. Few authors have considered the political history of the entire election, including the crucial events of the last month of the campaign. The analytic narrative that follows provides an overview of the election based on the many published works on the campaign and unpublished materials at the Lyndon B. Johnson Library.

Like most Americans in 1968, I experienced the events of that year through television. It was a time of recurrent shocks, intense emotions, and passionate judgments. Twenty-four years later I have tried to examine the election in a calm and judicious spirit. During a troubled time, fallible men and women made decisions that changed the nation. This book considers the reasons for actions and events that occurred during the critical 1968 election and the lasting consequences for American politics and society.

A Note on the Second Edition, 2010

In the more than sixteen years since *1968* first appeared, Bill Clinton, George W. Bush, and Barack Obama have occupied the White House. The Republicans recaptured Congress in 1994 and the Democrats did so in 2006. The rise of international terrorism and the events of September 11, 2001, the menace of global climate change, and the intense polarization of national politics have overshadowed the historical roots of the present condition of the United States. Yet the continuing readership of this book as a reliable, brief account of the election of 1968 suggested that an updated edition of the narrative would be useful for today's students of this significant moment in national politics.

I have left the basic structure of the book as it was in 1993. The prose has been tightened in spots; some quotations from figures such as Senator Edward M. Kennedy and Arthur M. Schlesinger, Jr., have been inserted; and errors have been corrected. The conclusion has been reshaped to reflect changes in American politics since the election of Bill Clinton in 1992 and to explain what happened to the main figures in the presidential race of 1968. The recommended reading has been updated to incorporate books that have appeared since the first edition.

Acknowledgments

I WANT TO THANK John Braeman and Ivan Dee for inviting me to contribute to the series of which this volume is a part. Both of them also offered helpful and thoughtful criticisms of earlier drafts. At the Lyndon Baines Johnson Library, Linda Hanson and Claudia Anderson provided their customary efficient and timely assistance. David Humphrey, then a staff member of the Library, directed me to information on the Vietnam negotiations that proved important for the final chapter.

My interest in this election grew out of an essay on Lyndon Johnson and the Democratic party that Robert A. Divine asked me to write. The late Herbert F. Margulies of the University of Hawaii provided informed and incisive comments on the entire manuscript. Students in seminars on Lyndon Johnson and his times helped me work out ideas on the politics of the 1960s. I owe special thanks to Thomas Clarkin, Byron Hulsey, Nancy Beck Young, and Mark Young for their kind assistance. Karen Gould was a constant source of encouragement through her good spirits and personal courage.

L. L. G.

January 2010
Austin, Texas

1968: The Election
That Changed America

Introduction

THE PRESIDENTIAL ELECTION of 1968 was a decisive event in twentieth-century American political history. After its victory in that contest, the Republican party dominated the White House through 2008, winning four of the next five presidential races by wide margins in the popular and electoral votes. After eight years of Bill Clinton and the Democrats, the Grand Old Party rebounded with the narrow victories of George W. Bush in 2000 and 2004. Only with the triumph of Barack Obama in 2008 did the Republican ascendancy appear to have come to an end.

For the Democrats, the picture at the presidential level turned bleak after 1968. In the twenty-four years after that contest, the Democrats were successful only in 1976 when a Southerner, Jimmy Carter, headed their ticket. Carter's narrow victory over Gerald Ford, a weak candidate in his own right, did not herald a Democratic revival. During the two decades that followed the 1968 race, Republicans set the agenda for American political life. The result was an ascendancy of conservative ideas and programs in the creation of national policy.

Until the mid-1960s the Democrats were the party of change and innovation. Beginning with Woodrow Wilson during the Progressive Era and continuing at an even greater rate with Franklin D. Roosevelt and the New Deal of the 1930s, the Democrats expanded the role of the national government in domestic and foreign policy. Roosevelt's Democratic successors, Harry S Truman, John F. Kennedy, and Lyndon B. Johnson, saw themselves as extending and elaborating the Roosevelt legacy.

Democratic power rested on an electoral base of a majority of American voters who made up what was called the New Deal coalition. As one Democrat noted during the 1960s, his party comprised "the liberal-labor-Negro coalition that has elected every liberal president and made possible every liberal advance since the 1930s." To most members of the party, Democrats were the natural governing organization of the nation. After all, with the exception of Dwight D. Eisenhower's eight years as president, Democrats had by 1964 controlled the White House for twenty-four of the preceding thirty-two years.

Between 1964 and 1968 the Democratic party lost ground. A number of elements explained this political decline. The presidential leadership of Lyndon B. Johnson alienated many voters who recoiled from the Great Society's domestic programs, the Democrats' racial liberalism, and the impact of the war in Vietnam. Within four years after Johnson's smashing triumph over Barry Goldwater and the Republicans in 1964, Democrats were beleaguered and discredited. Late in 1967 Postmaster General Lawrence F. O'Brien surveyed the condition of his party and reported to President Johnson, "The Democratic party, to a greater or lesser extent, has lost contact with the voters."

While Democrats floundered during the mid-1960s, Republicans rebuilt their organization after the debacle of 1964. The GOP was not as weak as it appeared at the time of Goldwater's defeat. Its base in the Midwest and Far West gave it the electoral resources it needed to survive a reverse such as 1964 and to regroup and wait for Democratic difficulties. In addition, despite Goldwater's national defeat, Republicans had won five Southern states in 1964. With the erosion of Democratic support under Johnson, Republicans were poised to regain the electoral dominance they had lost during the 1930s.

Complicating the Republican task in 1968 was the presence of a viable third-party candidate in the South in the person of the former governor of Alabama, George C. Wallace. A talented demagogue, Wallace had a knack for articulating the resentments and fears of white Americans, north and south, in rhetoric that assailed both major parties with equal venom. Both Republicans and Democrats were forced to conduct two-front political campaigns in 1968 to stave off the strong threat Wallace posed to the two-party system.

Most writing on the 1968 election has concentrated on the exciting events of that turbulent year—Lyndon Johnson's withdrawal in late March, the assassination of Martin Luther King, Jr., in early April and the killing of Senator Robert F. Kennedy in early June, and the tumultuous Democratic National Convention in August. These sensational occurrences made the election seem at the time a contest primarily for the soul of the Democratic party. The issue seemed to be how liberal the United States would be in the future. The outcome of the election, however, showed that the Democrats had indeed lost touch with the country.

Such an outcome would have seemed improbable to Democrats in November 1964. Lyndon Johnson had led his party to a sweeping triumph over the Republicans. The president carried all but six states and swamped Goldwater in the electoral college, 486 to 52. The gap in the popular vote total between the winner and the loser was 16 million ballots. And Johnson's coattails were long and effective. Democrats controlled the House of Representatives by 290 to 145 and the Senate by 68 to 32. The question at the time was whether Republicans had become a permanent minority that could no longer mount a credible challenge to the Democrats.

The Democratic triumph proved to be brief. Within two years Republicans rebounded and demonstrated that their obituaries had been premature. In the 1966 congressional elections the GOP gained forty-seven seats in the House and three in the Senate. They added eight governorships to those they already controlled. In the key state of California, newcomer Ronald Reagan achieved a decisive success. Richard Nixon recalled that his party "had been the recipient of a massive anti-Johnson windfall." What had happened in two years to transform Democratic triumph into a Republican comeback that presaged the party's return to the presidency in 1968? The presidential election of 1968 was determined in large measure by the decline in Democratic fortunes that occurred between 1964 and 1968.

Most explanations for the Democratic debacle have identified the Vietnam War as the major cause. Certainly fighting in Southeast Asia attracted most of the press attention during the campaign. Yet the most important subject on the minds of voters was race. The gains of blacks during the years 1960–1967 had aroused powerful resentment among the white population. Urban riots, student protests, and the rise of the Black Power movement further alienated whites. The result was an electoral reaction against Democrats that remained a powerful element in national politics for decades. A direct link exists between the character of the Nixon and Wallace campaigns in 1968 and the subsequent Republican campaigns of Ronald Reagan, George H. W. Bush, and George W. Bush. This salience of the race issue in 1968 made this electoral contest a decisive episode in national politics during the second half of the twentieth century.

1

On the Eve of 1968

THE PRESIDENTIAL ELECTION YEAR of 1968 began in a poisoned atmosphere of social tension and political bitterness. "I think that 1968 is going to be the worst year that any of us has seen here," said a British journalist based in New York as the New Year opened. American columnists and reporters echoed his gloomy prediction. "There is a sharp sense of crisis in the American air, spreading and souring," wrote Emmet John Hughes in *Newsweek*. Hughes found "a tension in society and a stress among men—not known since the 1930s."

The most immediate source of the pervasive unhappiness in the nation was the war in Vietnam. Since Lyndon Johnson had intensified the American commitment in Southeast Asia in 1965 with the bombing campaign against North Vietnam and the introduction into South Vietnam of large numbers of combat troops, the conflict had raged on with greater loss of life on both sides and with no tangible military gains. Almost half a million American soldiers were in Vietnam by the end of 1967. Casualties among Americans in the fighting had reached 150,000, with 20,000 deaths since 1961. The number of dead and wounded among the Vietnamese population stood in the millions. More and more Americans—over 40 percent in one poll—regarded the war as a mistake. Anti-war protests grew in size and intensity during the autumn of 1967. Demonstrators became more and more pointed in the denunciation of the man they saw as responsible for the endless carnage.

> Hey, hey, LBJ
> How many kids
> Did you kill today?

As the cruel rhyme indicated, Lyndon Baines Johnson aroused passions almost as heated as those surrounding the war. Johnson was entering the fifth year of his presidency. He had come to the White House upon the assassination of John F. Kennedy on November 22, 1963. During his first eighteen months in office the president had been a legislative dynamo, pushing through laws and advocating the creation of a "Great Society" which would conquer poverty and injustice. He had beaten Barry Goldwater in a landslide in the 1964 presidential election and seemed to stand atop American politics as his full term began in January 1965.

Despite his huge electoral triumph, the fifty-nine-year-old Johnson remained a mystery to many Americans. He had been a member of the House for eleven years and then won a disputed— some said "stolen"— election to the Senate in 1948 by an eighty-seven-vote majority in the Democratic primary. "Landslide Lyndon" rose rapidly in the Senate and became majority leader in 1955. His ability to enact measures such as the Civil Rights Act of 1957 made him a prominent national Democrat. After he lost the 1960 race for the Democratic presidential nomination, John F. Kennedy named him as his running mate. Johnson's years as vice president were unhappy ones, and rumors were heard that he might not be on the ticket in 1964. Then came Dallas and he was president.

Johnson seemed larger than life in the early days of his presidency. He was everywhere—on the phone to lawmakers, cajoling reporters, exhorting the nation to do great things. In the sad aftermath of Kennedy's death, he seemed a figure of calm authority who managed a seamless transition of power. His political appeal was one of "moderate and prudent" leadership, in the words of one newspaper correspondent. With his election to the presidency at stake, he sought "to preempt the high ground, the moderate thoroughfare, the middle of the road from his Republican opponents." The Lyndon Johnson whom Americans saw in 1964 was as dignified and restrained a man as it was possible for him to be.

Another, less attractive Lyndon Johnson emerged during the three years that followed. He treated staff members with a mixture of sadistic cruelty and benevolent paternalism that became legendary in Washington. To the press he was alternately solicitous and carping. He loved to deceive reporters in ways large and small. In an era before it was seemly to say the president lied, Johnson became known for his "credibility gap." As a reporter for *Time* put it, "He cannot stand affronts and regards his occasional critics as treasonous."

Johnson yearned to win the affection and trust of the American people, but the task proved beyond his powers. He had an essential insecurity at the center of his personality that prevented him from trusting his fellow citizens to sustain his policies on their merits. A close adviser, Joseph Califano, observed that Johnson "learned too late that the manipulative and devious behavior commonplace in the back alleys of legislative politics appalled the American people when exposed in their President." Johnson once asked a friend why people didn't like him. The answer was, "Mr. President, you are not a very likable man."

These drawbacks hampered Johnson even more as a wartime president. American involvement in Southeast Asia was substantial when John F. Kennedy was killed. Presidents Truman, Eisenhower, and Kennedy had committed the United States to oppose Vietnamese communism and after 1954 to support the new country of South Vietnam that had been created when France withdrew as a colonial power. During the Kennedy administration the number of American military "advisers" in South Vietnam rose from six hundred to sixteen thousand men at the time of the president's murder. Johnson had a valid if typically overstated point when he said in 1965 that "since 1954 every American president has offered support to the people of South Vietnam."

But Lyndon Johnson's presidential decisions had propelled the United States into the major combat phase of the war in Vietnam, and it became his significant political problem. If he took credit for the legislative accomplishments of his administration in domestic affairs, he could not evade responsibility for the Vietnam War that by late 1967 had become a foreign policy failure.

Johnson had asked Congress for authority to make bombing strikes after North Vietnamese naval vessels allegedly attacked American ships in the Gulf of Tonkin in 1964. He had decided to bomb North Vietnam on a sustained basis in early 1965, and later that year had sent large contingents of combat troops to South Vietnam. To most of the American public, the conflict, whatever its origins, had become "Lyndon Johnson's War."

The president had been unable to offer a convincing rationale for U.S. involvement in this Asian conflict. He had also failed to provide a clear statement of how Americans would know when victory had been achieved. These political troubles grew out of the confused purposes within the Johnson administration itself. There the war in Vietnam was seen as part of a larger confrontation between an expansionist Communist campaign, masterminded by the Soviet Union and Communist China and working through the North Vietnamese, and the forces of Western democracy seeking to preserve the independence of South Vietnam. At the same time Washington recognized that South Vietnam lacked the internal cohesion and national will to defeat its enemy. The United States aimed to overcome this political weakness through the use of its military power until South Vietnam could stand on its own. Many observers believed that the American presence undermined a faint South Vietnamese nationalism and defeated the very goal it sought to achieve. The United States was thus trying to prop up a country that appeared to lack the resolve to defend itself.

The Johnson administration also underestimated the will and determination of North Vietnam. Bombing raids were designed to inflict sufficient pain on the government in Hanoi so that it would either abandon efforts to subvert South Vietnam or agree to a negotiated political settlement. North Vietnam believed, however, that the United States lacked the will for a prolonged war. "Americans do not like long, inconclusive wars," said one North Vietnamese leader, "thus we are sure to win in the end." On their side, the North Vietnamese had Russian and Chinese logistical support, an agricultural country that bombing could injure but not destroy, and each year a hundred thousand young men who turned eighteen. Lyndon Johnson was fighting an enemy with the means and determination to conduct a long war. The administration could not supply a credible prediction of success.

By 1967 all the Johnson White House could offer to the people of the United States was continued bombing in North and South Vietnam, a steady increase in American dead and wounded, and an elusive promise that just a little more sacrifice and effort would show positive results. By the autumn of 1967 the patience of the American people with Johnson's policy was running out. On both sides of the war issue, sentiment grew for an end to the fighting. Advocates of peace, often called "doves," clamored for a negotiated settlement. Supporters of the war, labeled "hawks," asked why the war could not be won since the United States was expending so much blood and treasure. They argued for more intensive bombing even if it risked a confrontation with China.

The focus of the discontent over Vietnam was Johnson himself. Even Democrats now accused him "of the most monstrous character failings imaginable" in the conduct of the war. "He's got this Texan policy of shoot first and ask questions afterward," said one liberal critic. Republican governor Ronald Reagan of California charged Johnson with wasting American lives in the war. "He must take responsibility for the policy of war and what the results of that policy are." Reagan's answer was more vigorous prosecution of the fighting. By October 1967 the president's approval rating had fallen to a record low 31 percent. Johnson had told a reporter a few months earlier: "Our biggest problem is not with Ho [Chi Minh, the North Vietnamese leader] and with the fighting out there. It's with our situation here. It's leading the enemy to believe that we might quit."

Damaging as the Vietnam War was for Lyndon Johnson and the Democrats, it did not approach the impact on the American voter of an even more volatile domestic problem—the race issue. By August 1967 the White House was receiving public opinion polls indicating that "racial problems" were "the number one concern of 8 out of 10" of those surveyed. Taken during a period of urban rioting that marked the summer of 1967, this poll tracked other evidence of the same public mood. In 1966 surveys, three-quarters of the white electorate had said that blacks were moving ahead too fast. White voters contended that blacks demanded too much at the expense of whites. After Democratic losses in the 1966 congressional elections, organized labor discovered that many union members "deserted liberal candidates for one reason only: in protest against their advocacy of civil rights."

The civil rights record of Johnson's presidency was impressive. It included the Civil Rights Act of 1964, which gave all citizens equal access to public facilities irrespective of their race and outlawed racial discrimination in education and in the work-place. Next came the Voting Rights Act of 1965, which removed barriers to voting in the South. In the minds of Southern whites, the Johnson administration also implemented these policies with vigor. More than any other president before him, Johnson had identified his administration with the aspirations of blacks. In September 1966 he declared that "20 million of our Negro fellow citizens have the power of the United States government behind their right to vote for the first time in the history of this land."

By 1967, however, the Democratic record on civil rights had become a political liability. To militant blacks who advocated a stronger attack on racism, Johnson was at most an untrustworthy friend. At the other end of the political spectrum, many white voters saw the Johnson administration as sacrificing their inter-ests on behalf of blacks who responded to federal programs and money with violence and rioting. Two British politicians visiting the United States during the election of 1966 informed an aide of Vice President Hubert Humphrey that "in district after district, and city after city, they found an undercurrent of resentment concerning civil order and gains made by the Negro population."

A number of forces had produced this unhappy condition for the Democrats. Inside the civil rights movement, the nonviolent tactics of Dr. Martin Luther King, Jr., had proved less effective in dealing with racial conditions in Northern cities such as Chi-cago. Champions of a more assertive style of protest had gained national attention with calls for "Black Power" and a degree of separatism from white society. Beginning with riots in the Watts district of Los Angeles in 1965 and continuing in the "long, hot summers" of 1966 and 1967, urban violence had become part of the unfolding story of black protest against their disadvantaged place in American society. The result was a high degree of ap-prehension among whites about the direction of the civil rights movement and a mounting resentment at what they perceived as ingratitude among blacks for the sacrifices whites had made on their behalf.

In the popular mind, the state of race relations became connected to mounting protests against the war in Vietnam. The resulting social trauma provided evidence that the Johnson administration was insensitive to issues of "law and order" and unwilling to take a tough stand against domestic dissent. The president, according to this view, was responsible for calling forth the protests and then for allowing them to continue. "Disturbances and demonstrations are lumped together," argued one White House memorandum, "and the blame for these civil disorders is placed on the Administration."

The issue of crime and citizen safety worked against the party in power. During the 1960s the incidence of violent crimes—murder, rapes, assaults, and robberies—had increased at an alarming rate. Over the first six years of the decade, the number of reported crimes rose by more than 60 percent while the population grew only 10 percent. Between 1960 and 1970 the rate at which blacks were arrested for homicide rose by more than 130 percent. Campaigning for president in 1968, Richard Nixon charged that during the Johnson administration "crime and violence have increased ten times faster than the population." These alarming allegations oversimplified a more complex reality to which demographic shifts, the availability of firearms, and the tensions of urban living contributed. Nonetheless the crime issue became a continuing burden for the Johnson White House and the Democrats.

One popular explanation for the rising crime rate was that liberal judges imposed restrictions on police officers in the performance of their duties. The U.S. Supreme Court, led by Chief Justice Earl Warren, received primary blame or credit for this situation. The Court's decision in *Miranda v. Arizona* (1966), requiring police to inform a suspect in a criminal case of the right to remain silent during questioning, symbolized what many believed to be an undue sensitivity to the rights of criminals rather than their victims. In fact the *Miranda* decision did not frustrate the police to the extent that its critics charged, but the perception during the 1960s was that it did. Judges whom Lyndon Johnson had nominated for the Supreme Court, particularly his old friend Abe Fortas, were the focus of conservative attacks for their rulings on criminal procedures. Fortas's role in the *Miranda* case, said Senator Sam Ervin, Democrat of North Carolina, had allowed "multitudes of murderers, rapists, burglars, robbers, and thieves to go unwhipped of justice." The law-and-order issue nagged at the Democrats all during the 1968 campaign.

On the surface the economy should not have been a problem for the White House as the presidential race neared. Unemployment during 1967 had been around 4 percent, and inflation was running at under 3 percent annually. The projected deficit in the federal budget for 1968 would be more than $11 billion. Although economic activity had been sluggish in 1967, the economy was still enjoying the boom of the 1960s. Defense spending on the Vietnam War was further accelerating economic growth.

In the politics of 1968, however, these optimistic figures masked a more difficult reality. Although inflation was still low compared to what the 1970s and 1980s would bring, the rise in prices worried voters, and they told pollsters it was their "most urgent problem." The projected budget deficit was quite large by the standards of the time, and Republicans charged that it reflected the distorted priorities of the Johnson administration in advancing domestic programs during wartime. There were also fears for the stability of the dollar in international markets during 1967–1968. The balance of payments was running against the United States, and gold was leaving the country. The financial impact of the war in Vietnam was disrupting the federal budget, unleashing inflation, and calling into question President Johnson's management of the economy.

The administration also encountered substantial economic discontent among the nation's farmers. In May 1967 aides of Vice President Humphrey told the White House that the Democrats would likely lose "every non-southern state with a farm-voter population of 9% or more." The agricultural community in the Midwest complained that their expenses rose constantly while the prices they received for their crops had fallen off since 1966. Advocates for the farmer charged that during a time of prosperity, "people out in the country are earning lower incomes than big-city minority slum dwellers." Farmers blamed the Johnson administration for "holding down consumer food prices at the farmer's expense." When the White House endorsed cheaper food prices and the president urged housewives not to buy expensive butter, Democrats suffered in the farm belt.

Added to these substantive issues was the Democratic organizational disarray after four years of Johnson's political leadership. Despite the president's reputation as a masterful politician, in fact he had little interest in the workings of the party machinery. The Democratic National Committee had withered during his presidency. Its chairman, John Bailey of Connecticut, was a figurehead; Johnson kept real power in his own hands. He shifted fund-raising to large contributors and allowed the party's base of small donors to dry up. Almost no attention went to such basic matters as voter registration and mobilization. Seeking to be a nonpartisan president, Johnson made appointments in many states without regard to party affiliation, to the dismay of committed Democrats. As Postmaster General Lawrence O'Brien warned Johnson in September 1967, the result was that "many of the state organizations are flabby and wedded to techniques which are conventional and outmoded." In addition, "The Democratic National Committee is not staffed or equipped to conduct a successful presidential election."

So striking were Lyndon Johnson's political problems in late 1967 that he faced the unusual situation for an incumbent president of an important challenge to his renomination. By December 1967 Johnson had a declared opponent in the field against him and another potential rival of even greater significance. The announced contender was Senator Eugene J. McCarthy of Minnesota, who had become a candidate on November 30. He said he would enter several primaries "to challenge the President's position" on Vietnam, and he contended that his campaign did not represent "any great threat to the unity and strength of the Democratic party." The other possible rival was Senator Robert F. Kennedy of New York, brother of the late president. During the last months of 1967 Kennedy had been seriously weighing a race against the president but had decided not to make the run under the existing circumstances.

When McCarthy announced, the political consensus was that he posed no serious threat to Lyndon Johnson's renomination in 1968. How could a relatively obscure senator from the upper Midwest defeat an incumbent president for renomination? When the McCarthy campaign got off to a slow start, the conventional wisdom was reinforced. By mid-December 1967, a White House aide informed the president with amusement that "Eugene McCarthy is doing so badly that I am tempted to float a rumor that he is actually working for you to dispirit the 'peace movement.'" Reports from around the country supported a discounting of McCarthy's chances.

In fact the McCarthy revolt against the president represented a more important political threat than the White House realized. Throughout the early months of 1968 most political observers underestimated McCarthy's capacity as a candidate.

This misjudgment grew out of his mixed record as a senator since 1958. Fifty-two years old in 1968, McCarthy had won election to the House of Representatives in 1950 and served four terms. In 1958 he ran for the Senate against a popular Republican and won a large victory in the Democratic landslide that year. He was an effective liberal legislator during his first term. His talents led Johnson to consider him as a serious vice-presidential possibility in 1964; as a liberal and a Catholic, McCarthy would have balanced the ticket well.

In the end, Johnson decided that Hubert Humphrey had even better claims on the position because of his liberal accomplishments and standing within the Democratic party. The process by which Johnson led McCarthy on and then dumped him in favor of Humphrey left some scars with the senator who was a proud, even conceited figure. Surveying the possible Democratic candidates in 1960, for example, McCarthy had quipped, "Why don't they just nominate me. I'm twice as liberal as Humphrey, twice as Catholic as Kennedy, and twice as smart as [Stuart] Symington." For a man of McCarthy's self-esteem, to be turned down in favor of his Minnesota colleague, whom he regarded as inferior, was a wound that smarted for years. "He really felt he was led down the primrose path," a relative later recalled.

McCarthy's willingness to challenge Johnson in 1968 did not rest simply on a personality conflict with the president. It also arose from McCarthy's reservations about the wisdom of the administration's Vietnam policy and the view of the presidency that Johnson advanced to support his actions. An initial break came during 1965 when the administration intervened in the Dominican Republic to put down an ostensible Communist government in that Latin American country. By January 1966 McCarthy was also attacking the Vietnam War. So serious was the commitment of American power, he said, that it required "a national debate, a national discussion, and a real searching of the mind and soul of America." He did not move to outright opposition to the president until 1967. On February 1 he told an audience at a peace mobilization in Washington that in the absence of positive reasons for supporting the conflict "we must be prepared to pass harsh and severe judgment on our position in this war." Four weeks later he called the war "morally unjustifiable."

Several elements led McCarthy to this position. His daughter Mary was a convinced opponent of the fighting, and in 1966 and 1967 she had a strong influence on her father's thinking. The actions of the Johnson administration, and its constitutional rationale for the war, also troubled the Minnesota senator. He doubted the argument that China needed to be contained, and it bothered him when the Gulf of Tonkin Resolution of 1964 was invoked to justify the president's policy. After Undersecretary of State Nicholas Katzenbach called the resolution the "functional equivalent" of a declaration of war, an angry McCarthy told a reporter, "There is no limit to what he says the president can do. There is only one thing to do—take it to the country." A suspicion of imperial presidents and their actions would be a significant theme in McCarthy's campaign in 1968.

By early 1967 McCarthy was beginning to think about mounting a challenge to Johnson, if only to provoke a debate on the wisdom of the Vietnam policy. The most formidable obstacle to such a move was Senator Robert F. Kennedy of New York, the heir apparent to his brother's political legacy. If Kennedy decided to run against Johnson, McCarthy's chances would disappear. During the autumn of 1967, however, it seemed that Kennedy was reluctant to go up against an incumbent president, and opponents of Johnson turned to other alternatives. McCarthy's possible candidacy took on new allure.

Within the left wing of the Democratic party there had been rumbles all during 1967 of challenging Lyndon Johnson's candidacy. The leading proponents of what became the "Dump

Johnson" effort were two opponents of the war, Allard K. Lowenstein and Curtis Gans. Lowenstein had been active in liberal
causes since his college days and had participated in the Adlai
Stevenson campaigns of the 1950s. During the 1960s he had
played a role in civil rights campaigns and was an official of the
Americans for Democratic Action (ADA). Gans was also a member of the ADA and had earlier been connected with the more
militant Students for a Democratic Society (SDS). In July 1967
Gans made Johnson the target of an insurgent political movement which would run candidates against him in the 1968 primaries. If all went well, Gans contended, Johnson might decide
to withdraw from the race, as President Harry S Truman had
done in 1952. During the remainder of the summer and into the
fall, Lowenstein and Gans used a shadow organization, the Conference for Concerned Democrats, to find an alternative to the
president. They found stirrings of support among liberal Democrats opposed to the war.

Their first choice was Robert Kennedy, but after a series of
meetings in September and October 1967 the New York senator
declined. "People would say that I was splitting the party out of
ambition and envy," Kennedy told them. Other possibilities, including Senator George McGovern of South Dakota, stood aside.
In mid-October Lowenstein went to see McCarthy and found to
his surprise that the senator was willing. "Somebody has to raise
the flag," McCarthy remarked. Six days later, in a meeting with
Lowenstein and another liberal leader, McCarthy made his decision definite. "You guys have been talking about three or four
names. I think you can cut the list down to one now."

McCarthy proved to be a formidable candidate, but he did
not seem so at first. His second term in the Senate had not been a
distinguished one, in part because he had become bored with the
routine of the place. His voting record on several issues revealed
vulnerabilities that his opponents would exploit during 1968. He

had voted for the oil depletion allowance that favored the oil industry; his civil rights record was solid but seemed to lack the emotional sympathy for black aspirations that Robert Kennedy now displayed. He wanted to run for president in his own way and on his own terms. The McCarthy campaign was always disorganized and confused, and in his formal speeches the candidate rarely stirred his listeners.

On the other hand, McCarthy's understated style was appealing to the group within the Democratic party that remembered with affection the campaigns of Adlai Stevenson. There was about McCarthy much that resonated with liberals in the suburbs who expected candidates to make rational arguments on serious issues. His laconic wit also evoked memories of John F. Kennedy's personal style. The senator drew on the support of independents and some Republicans who responded to his wry, literate speeches and his detached, ironic approach to public life. He was uncomfortable asking for the votes of Americans on the basis of ethnic affiliation or economic position. His base, he said, was "a constituency of conscience."

McCarthy intended to run in four primaries—Massachusetts, Wisconsin, Oregon, and California—where his anti-war message would have the greatest appeal. Supporters urged him also to run in the bellwether New Hampshire primary on March 12, 1968, but throughout December 1967 the senator weighed the wisdom of such a move. On January 3 he announced that he would enter the New Hampshire contest. The chairman of the Democratic National Committee warned the White House that the McCarthy forces would pose a real threat to the president in both Massachusetts and New Hampshire.

For Lyndon Johnson and the men around him, McCarthy's opposition was considered to be less of a threat than the possible challenge from Robert Kennedy. The president and the New York senator had long detested each other. Their animosity went back at least to the 1960 campaign when Kennedy had managed his brother's presidential race in a manner that alienated Lyndon Johnson. During Johnson's time as vice president, their dislike for each other had intensified. A year of uneasy collaboration followed Johnson's assumption of the presidency in 1963; the two men had maintained a charade of public unity. The president rebuffed efforts to have Kennedy become his running mate, but he supported his former attorney general's Senate candidacy in New York. During 1965 and 1966 Kennedy moved cautiously away from his endorsement of Johnson's policy on Vietnam. In early 1967 he came out against the bombing of North Vietnam and called for negotiations with Hanoi toward a resolution of the conflict.

Kennedy was the logical leader of the anti-war forces within the Democratic party. Only he had the electoral appeal to mount a credible challenge to Johnson's candidacy for renomination. If he ran, he would evoke the memory of his assassinated brother. Kennedy's standing with black Americans, the young, and the disadvantaged led many Democrats to regard him as a potential healer for the tensions roiling American society. It was an attractive vision for many in the party who dreamed that such a coalition might ensure a Democratic victory in the fall.

The New York senator was a shrewd enough politician to recognize the weaknesses of his possible candidacy. In the South he was an object of hatred among many whites, and his candidacy in Dixie would be hard to sustain. Within Democratic ranks he had a well-deserved reputation for playing hardball politics, and a challenge to Johnson would be seen as further confirmation of his limitless ambition. If he went up against the president and lost, he would impair his chances for a future race for the White House. The death of his brother had hit Robert Kennedy hard, and he was reluctant to take on the rigors of a presidential contest with its dangers and burdens for his family. Dislike of

Johnson and the Vietnam War impelled him to run, but caution stayed his hand. "In his gut, he wanted to go," a friend remembered. "He felt it was the right thing to do, but his judgment told him his chances were so slim, it wasn't the right decision."

When Lowenstein and Gans approached Kennedy in the autumn of 1967, he turned them down. It was a significant mistake. Kennedy had judged that Johnson would remain politically strong and that no other Democrat could mount a credible opposition to the president. When McCarthy entered the race, the action suggested that the Minnesota senator had the courage to run while Kennedy, the exponent of moral values and passion in politics, stood aside. The contrast that young people and antiwar activists drew between the two men did not please Kennedy, but he continued to believe as 1968 opened that he should stay out of the presidential race.

On the eve of the presidential contest in 1968, the Democratic party stood in feeble condition. Its electoral base was tottering, its hold on the voters was slipping, its internal organization was chaotic. Many voters disliked Johnson. The policies of his administration had made converts for his partisan opposition. As a result, Johnson's candidacy in 1968, though not yet announced, had already drawn one potentially credible rival in Eugene McCarthy. Meanwhile Robert Kennedy waited just offstage.

Victory for the Democrats in 1968 rested, party members told one another, on the anticipated mistakes of the Republicans. In this comforting scenario, the GOP would nominate Richard Nixon, a sure loser. Second, the presence of George C. Wallace of Alabama as a third-party candidate would "drain enough votes from the Republicans to elect Johnson." In essence the Democrats would not have to win the 1968 election. Their opponents would lose it.

The Republican party did not intend to be so obliging. The election of 1964 had been a political debacle for the GOP. As a

Republican governor put it in December 1964, "we have suffered a defeat as severe in quality and quantity as any that the
Republican party has ever sustained." In addition to losing the
presidency, the Republicans had dropped 38 seats in the House
of Representatives to stand at 140 members, lowest since 1936.
In the Senate they had lost two seats and had only 32 members,
which put them where they had been in 1940. More Republican
defeats in state and local contests prompted talk of the eventual
disappearance of the party from the American political scene.

Republican rebuilding began in January 1965 with the selection of a new chairman of the Republican National Committee.
Ray Bliss was a veteran party leader from Ohio where he had assembled an effective statewide organization. In 1960 Bliss's skill
had enabled Richard Nixon to carry Ohio against the popularity
of John F. Kennedy. Still, the task he confronted when he took
over the RNC in early 1965 was staggering. The Goldwater defeat had left the party in disarray, though there was some good
news on finances because of late contributions the party received
in 1964. Bliss persuaded the holdover Goldwater supporters
on the committee to leave, and he turned to fund-raising on a
sustained basis. Success on the financial side came as party contributors, large and small, poured in enough money to make the
Republicans competitive in the 1966 elections. Bliss also stressed
organization rather than ideology and rebuilt the party's organizational base. He allowed the Republican Coordinating Committee, composed of officeholders and party leaders, to frame
alternatives to Johnson's programs. Bliss concentrated on the issue of inflation, and that bread-and-butter subject emerged as a
chief talking point in the Republican rebound.

Events also worked in the Republicans' favor. The popular
reaction against Great Society programs in 1965 and 1966 made
the electorate more sympathetic to the Republican message. Most
significant were the issues of race and crime. In a September

1966 poll 52 percent of Americans thought the Johnson administration was moving too fast on civil rights.

The 1966 congressional elections indicated how the administration had lost ground among voters. Republicans picked up forty-seven seats in the House of Representatives and gained three senators and eight new governors. The number of Americans identifying themselves as Republican rose from 25 to 29 percent, reversing twenty years of decline. New GOP faces appeared—Charles S. Percy won a Senate seat in Illinois when he defeated a liberal stalwart, Paul H. Douglas; Spiro Agnew became the new governor of Maryland; and in California the popular and attractive Ronald Reagan trounced the Democratic incumbent, Edmund G. "Pat" Brown. Republicans were no longer political invalids; they were credible challengers to Lyndon Johnson and the Democrats in 1968.

The next step for Republicans, however, was more difficult: they needed a nominee to run against Lyndon Johnson in the presidential race. The ostensible front-runner after 1966 was the governor of Michigan, George Romney. Elected to three terms in a key industrial state, Romney was a handsome, imposing figure on television. A former automobile executive and a devout Mormon, he seemed to have an appealing blend of business experience and executive ability. Reporters familiar with his career in Michigan wondered how well his ponderous speaking style and slow-moving mind would fare on the national scene. Another potential contender was Nelson A. Rockefeller, governor of New York. Barry Goldwater's main opponent in 1964, Rockefeller had incurred the hatred of the party's conservative wing for his attacks on their hero. Finally, a third governor was Ronald Reagan, whose victory in California had been large and decisive. A staunch supporter of Goldwater, Reagan had already shown an ability to captivate conservative audiences, and his advisers were eying a race in 1968.

The most formidable entrant in the Republican race was a man who had been widely regarded as a political has-been only a few years earlier. Richard Milhous Nixon was fifty-three in 1966; he had been an important participant in American politics for a decade and a half. After eight years as Eisenhower's vice president, he lost the 1960 presidential election to John F. Kennedy in a close and hard-fought contest. Attempting a comeback two years later by running for governor of California, he lost again to Edmund G. Brown. Some in the press then wrote Nixon's political obituary. In 1964 he remained loyal to Goldwater when other Republicans such as Rockefeller wavered. Once Johnson's policies faltered, Nixon was ready to court the Republican faithful once again. In 1966 he campaigned eagerly for party candidates across the country, amassing the credits he would turn into delegate votes in 1968.

So successful had Nixon been as a surrogate campaigner for Republicans in 1966 that Lyndon Johnson attacked him on the eve of the congressional voting. After the Republican criticized his Vietnam policy, Johnson called Nixon "a chronic campaigner." Nixon exploited this opportunity with his customary partisan skill. He styled it "one of the most savage personal assaults ever leveled by the President of the United States against one of his political opponents," adding that Johnson's comments were those of a "very, very tired man." The exchange reminded voters of Nixon's stature among Republicans and enabled him to treat the party's election victory as something of a personal triumph as well.

During 1967 Nixon assembled a campaign operation that was efficient and well financed. While the candidate stepped back from politics for the first half of the year and made a series of foreign tours, the men around him framed a strategy for the campaign ahead. Nixon's main problem was his image as a "loser," derived from the 1960 and 1962 defeats. He decided he had to contest the Republican primaries to prove his appeal to the voters. Meanwhile his standing in the polls against the president improved.

In late 1967, moreover, one of Nixon's potential rivals, George Romney, had inflicted a mortal wound on his own campaign. In a television interview after a trip to Vietnam, Romney was asked about how his position on the war had changed. He replied that "when I came back from Vietnam, I just had the greatest brainwashing that anybody can get when you go over to Vietnam, not only by the generals but also by the diplomatic corps over there." As the episode became public it suggested that Romney's brain was not up to the job of being president. Soon his campaign began to falter for lack of support and money. Polls by the Romney campaign in December 1967 showed him trailing Nixon by more than fifty percentage points. The Romney presidential bid was over, and on February 26, 1968, he took himself out of the race.

Two potential threats remained for Nixon as 1968 opened. If Nelson Rockefeller entered the contest, his money and energy might win some support. But the Nixon campaign was confident that Rockefeller lacked the strength among Republican partisans to make a serious challenge. More formidable was the new Republican governor of California, Ronald Reagan. While Reagan had pledged to voters during his gubernatorial race that he would not run for the White House, he had not said that he would refuse a draft. During 1967 a number of conservative political operatives began putting together a Reagan-for-President campaign. Already a popular speaker before Republican audiences, Reagan spent much of the year on the banquet circuit with five-by-eight note cards that carried his prepared text. His one-liners delighted his audiences. "You have to admire the Administration's crime program. They're making the money so cheap it's not worth stealing." If Reagan were to enter the race, he could give the Nixon campaign some anxious weeks.

If the 1968 election had simply matched the Republican and Democratic candidates, it would not have produced the complexity and passion that prevailed throughout that tumultuous year. What helped to set this presidential race apart was the presence of a serious third-party candidate, the former governor of Alabama, George Corley Wallace. Wallace's talent for exploiting the racial tensions within the electorate and articulating the grievances of middle-class and lower-middle-class white voters made him a force that confounded the plans and projects of Republicans and Democrats alike. Wallace did not inject the race issue into the 1968 contest, but he used it with explosive effectiveness.

George Wallace had served as governor of Alabama from 1963 through 1967. In his inaugural address he had proclaimed, "Segregation now! Segregation tomorrow! Segregation forever!" and he had tried to block the efforts of the federal government to integrate his state's colleges and universities. In one celebrated and well-publicized episode, he stood in the door of a building at the University of Alabama to bar black students from entering. Federal marshals made sure the students were admitted, but Wallace received nationwide notoriety for his tactic. By 1964 he had decided to run in some Democratic primaries to test his strength as a national candidate. To the surprise of many observers, he achieved respectable totals—34 percent of the vote in Wisconsin against President Johnson, 38 percent in the Indiana primary, and 43 percent in Maryland. In the wake of Johnson's landslide, worries about the "white backlash" that Wallace represented receded for a time, but the governor of Alabama was biding his moment until the 1968 race.

First he had to overcome a problem in his home state. Alabama law barred the governor from seeking a second term. Efforts to persuade the Alabama legislature to change the state constitution failed. Wallace got around the constitutional obstacle by having his wife, Lurleen, run to succeed him. After her election in November 1966, Wallace and the men around him turned to the formidable task of mounting a serious third-party challenge for the presidency. He raised about a million dollars in campaign funds during the first half of 1967, then sent his operatives to California to begin the difficult process of persuading voters in as many states as possible to put his name on the ballot. These efforts cost Wallace about half a million dollars, but by early 1968 he had succeeded. Across the South there was popular enthusiasm for the Wallace cause, and in all states in the North there was enough support to ensure that he would appear on the ballot.

What was Wallace's message in 1968? Race, he told reporters, was not the issue that drove his campaign. "There isn't any backlash among the mass of people against anybody because of color. There's a backlash against big government in this country," he said in 1967. To cheering audiences he would proclaim, "Our lives are being taken over by bureaucrats, and most of them have beards!" Wallace was careful not to make an overly racist appeal, but the language he used conveyed an unmistakable message to white audiences. On the volatile issue of busing school children to achieve integration, he assured the people, "When I become President there won't be one thin dime available from Federal funds to pay for all this school busin'—you can rely on that." For the members of the lower middle class in the North, "the average man in the street, the man in the textile mill, this man in the steel mill, this barber, the beautician, the policeman on the beat," Wallace was a candidate who spoke to their anxieties and fears. As a New York construction worker put it, there should be "one law for the Negro *and* the working man *and* the rich liberals. I think Wallace will do that."

The United States approached the presidential election year of 1968 in a condition of unusual political turbulence and uncertainty. Racial turmoil, economic unease, and the war in Vietnam had raised such tensions within the country during 1966 and 1967 that the presidential contest became an outlet for venting the accumulated frustrations of the decade. The American political system was about to endure a year that would test the strength and durability of its institutions. In the process, the nature of national politics would undergo long-lasting changes.

2

The President Withdraws

ON MARCH 31, 1968, Lyndon Johnson concluded a television address to the nation with the stunning announcement that he would not accept his party's nomination for president. Since that event several theories have emerged to explain why the most political president of his time suddenly abandoned national politics during an election year. The interlocking forces of Johnson's health, the war in Vietnam, and the dissenting challenges he faced within his own party combined to produce the president's decision to step down.

The question of his health during a second full term had long been on Johnson's mind. He knew that male members of his family rarely lived past sixty-five—which he would be in August 1973. The heart attack he had suffered in 1955 demanded that he live prudently, but there was always the possibility of another attack. He experienced gall bladder problems in 1965 and had an operation for skin cancer later in his presidency. His wife, Claudia "Lady Bird," doubted whether he could survive another term. When Johnson had talked about not running in 1964, just before the Democratic National Convention, she had urged him to continue in the race. By 1967, however, she was convinced that another term would expose him to dangerous health risks. She feared he might be stricken in office as Woodrow Wilson had been in 1919.

Discussions between husband and wife about a withdrawal from politics intensified during the autumn of 1967. As 1968 began they returned to the issue during a visit with Texas governor John Connally and his wife at the president's ranch in Texas. For a time Johnson planned an announcement at the close of his State of the Union Address on January 17, 1968. Either by accident or by design, the president failed to bring the statement with him, and the moment passed.

Johnson later said he probably would not have read the withdrawal statement anyway—it would have been a discordant note amidst his call for sacrifices in Vietnam and in domestic policy. The political situation also may have struck Johnson as more favorable to his administration and reelection than had been the case for several months. His poll ratings had improved since November. The campaign of Senator Eugene McCarthy had begun slowly. A poll commissioned by the White House and taken in late December showed the president with a seventy-percentage-point lead over McCarthy. Another poll gave McCarthy only 12 percent support in January. Anti-war Democrats complained that the McCarthy "campaign is a disaster"; the candidate's speeches were "dull, vague, and without either balls or poetry."

The president also had some reason for confidence in the outcome of the fall election. He learned on the afternoon of the State of the Union speech that the next Gallup poll would show him "with a big lead over Reagan, Romney and Nixon and a six-point leader over Rockefeller." Even though John Connally urged him to make the withdrawal announcement because "the longer you wait the more difficult it becomes," Johnson elected to wait a little longer.

The president had miscalculated; events soon turned against him. Four days after the speech the battle of Khe Sanh broke out near the Demilitarized Zone (DMZ) in South Vietnam. Johnson followed the fighting closely, believing that the engagement might be a climactic battle of the war. Then, on January 23, 1968, the North Koreans captured the *USS Pueblo*, an intelligence vessel, on the high seas, with its crew of eighty-three men. Bogged down in Vietnam, it seemed that the United States might be facing still another military confrontation. In Congress there was pressure to retaliate.

The most devastating military development for the president came on January 31. Across South Vietnam the North Vietnamese and their guerrilla supporters in the South launched what has become known as the Tet offensive, timed for the Vietnamese New Year. Americans saw vivid television footage of the United States embassy under assault in Saigon, American dead lying in the streets of their ally, and house-to-house fighting near U.S. bases. For Americans these were troubling images after constant reassurances from the Johnson administration about the prospects of victory.

The North Vietnamese offensive was defeated with heavy losses to the enemy—casualties in the tens of thousands—and their hopes for a popular uprising in the South went unrealized. In domestic political terms in the United States, the military outcome of the Tet offensive was less important than the shock it inflicted on American public opinion. Media coverage suggested that the nation had suffered a worse military defeat than was in fact the case.

The White House failed to depict the fighting as a setback for the enemy. As Senator George Aiken, a Vermont Republican, said of the administration's efforts to lessen the impact of the battle, "If this is failure, I hope the Viet Cong never have a major success." More ominous for the president was the campaign remark of Senator McCarthy. "Only a few months ago we were told that 65 percent of the population was secure. Now we know that even the American embassy is not secure." A week later Senator Robert Kennedy offered a more somber assessment: the

enemy in Vietnam had "finally shattered the mask of official il-
lusion with which we have concealed our true circumstances
from ourselves."

The Tet offensive shifted the ground of American politics.
In New Hampshire the McCarthy campaign gathered momentum as both defenders and opponents of the war turned against
the president's policies for their own reasons. As it turned out,
New Hampshire proved to be receptive to McCarthy's appeal
once Johnson seemed vulnerable. It was a small state with relatively few Democrats, and these could be reached by the kind
of intensive, personal campaign that McCarthy was mounting.
By early February the candidate had at his disposal an army of
student workers who had poured into the state to defeat Lyndon
Johnson. Shaving their beards to be "Clean for Gene," young
men spread out for door-to-door canvassing that played to the
love of personal contact among the New Hampshire voters. The
theme of their canvass was not explicitly anti-war. Instead the
McCarthy campaign said, "New Hampshire can bring America
back to its senses."

The Johnson campaign in New Hampshire played into the
hands of the McCarthy forces. Relying on the Democratic party
organization in the state, the Johnson people enlisted the support of Governor John King and Senator Thomas McIntyre.
A prominent businessman directed the Johnson effort. To preserve the fiction that the president was not yet an official candidate, the Johnson apparatus worked to obtain write-in votes for
him. As a means of tracking the allegiance of Johnson voters, his
campaign managers came up with the idea of a "pledge card"
that registered voters could fill in. Each card was numbered;
one section went to the White House and another to Johnson
headquarters. The McCarthy campaign immediately charged
that the pledge cards interfered with a secret ballot. The Johnson operation further overreached when its leaders claimed that

a vote for McCarthy was a vote for the North Vietnamese leader Ho Chi Minh. The reporter Charles Bartlett warned the president that McCarthy could get "a sympathy vote" if "these irritations accumulate."

A reminder of the nation's domestic difficulties appeared at the end of February. In response to urban riots in the summer of 1967, Johnson had named a national commission, led by Mayor John Lindsay of New York and Governor Otto Kerner of Illinois, to probe the causes of unrest. The Kerner Commission issued its report on February 29 and spoke of a nation "moving toward two societies, one black, one white—separate and unequal." The president's reaction to the report was restrained; he indicated that he "did not agree with all of the recommendations" of the panel. Johnson's response led Robert Kennedy to conclude "that he's not going to do anything about the war and he's not going to do anything about the cities either."

Two days before the New Hampshire voting, the *New York Times* reported that General William Westmoreland, commander of United States forces in South Vietnam, was asking for 206,000 more troops. According to the *Times*, the request had set off "a divisive internal debate" within the administration over whether or not to meet the request. The story was accurate, and the argument within the White House would prove important in Johnson's subsequent withdrawal from the campaign. Coming when it did, however, the *Times* story suggested that the administration was as likely to escalate the American commitment as it was to reduce it.

The result in New Hampshire surprised Washington. Although Johnson emerged the winner with 27,243 votes to 23,280 votes for McCarthy in the Democratic primary, the closeness of the race was unexpected. McCarthy also received some 4,700 votes in the Republican primary while Johnson got 1,778 Republican votes. Among the Democrats, Johnson's percentage of the vote was 49.4 percent while McCarthy received 42.2 percent. For an incumbent president seeking reelection, a narrow victory over a relatively unknown challenger was a shock. McCarthy won 20 of the 24 delegates at stake in the primary because the Johnson campaign, confident of victory, had put up more delegate candidates than places available. The more focused McCarthy campaign took the bulk of the national convention delegates. McCarthy had exceeded the expectations that the press had established for his campaign; Johnson had failed to live up to his reputation as a skillful politician. The New Hampshire results punctured the assumption that Lyndon Johnson was an unbeatable choice for the Democratic nomination.

The Republican primary outcome in New Hampshire was more decisive. Richard Nixon achieved an overwhelming victory with 84,005 votes to Nelson Rockefeller's 11,691. After George Romney's withdrawal from the race on February 28, 1968, the Nixon camp had feared that the significance of their candidate's showing might be ignored. Instead the triumph helped dispel the "loser" image that had dogged Nixon since 1962. It showed that he was a broad popular choice among Republicans who wanted to win in 1968. Earlier the press had viewed Rockefeller as Nixon's main competition because of the New Yorker's good showing against Johnson in the polls. In fact few conservative Republicans outside the Northeast had any stomach for Rockefeller. Nixon's most serious rival was the still unannounced Ronald Reagan.

During the New Hampshire primary Nixon evolved his own position on the Vietnam War. During a speech on March 5 he said he would offer "new leadership" to "end the war and win the peace in the Pacific." The press concluded that Nixon had a "secret plan" to end the war in Vietnam. Nixon had avoided being that explicit, but he did suggest that "the war can be ended if we mobilize our economic and political and diplomatic leadership." What he had in mind were diplomatic overtures by the United States to the Soviet Union and China to achieve a negotiated solution. Meanwhile American troops would be gradually withdrawn and more fighting left to the South Vietnamese. Beyond that Nixon refused to go, he said, because he did not wish to interfere with Johnson's foreign policy or tie his own hands if and when he became president. The position had enough ambiguity in it to satisfy critics of Johnson on both the left and the right, which was what Nixon intended.

The furor over Nixon's Vietnam program somewhat obscured the campaign themes he was developing in New Hampshire. He criticized those who led urban riots and urged action to forestall "planners of violence." As his rationale for providing new leadership, he cited "rampant lawlessness" and "racial strife" as well as economic decline and the war in Southeast Asia. Americans had "learned the hard way that a society that is lenient and permissive for criminals is a society that is neither safe nor secure for innocent men and women."

During the New Hampshire race Nixon also put in place the campaign style he would continue during the fall election. Still bitter at his treatment by the press during his 1960 race against John F. Kennedy and determined to prevent the media from influencing his themes, he and his aides gave few press conferences and relied on staged events aimed at the television cameras. Nixon made particularly adept use of question-and-answer sessions with ordinary citizens. In the process he convinced some journalists that a "New Nixon" had emerged—a cooler and less impulsive man than the candidate of the 1950s and early 1960s. As one of his aides said, "It's not the man we have to change, but rather the *received impression*." Nixon's success in this transformation would be an important element in his victory in 1968.

In the aftermath of New Hampshire many commentators attributed McCarthy's strong showing to displeasure with the

Johnson administration's Vietnam policy. There was some truth in this conclusion, but the anti-Johnson sentiment did not reflect support for the dovish position on Vietnam. One preelection poll indicated that "40 percent of those declaring for McCarthy also favored escalation" of the war. Many Democratic voters were registering a protest against the president for not *winning* the war in Vietnam; they were not against the conflict itself. Unhappiness with Johnson as a national leader and the "social issues" of race and crime were other elements in the vote against him.

The New Hampshire primary made Eugene McCarthy a credible national figure among Democrats. His campaign seemed likely to acquire that elusive quality of momentum that can be so important in a presidential race. He had already shown strength in other states where liberal Democrats were strong. In Massachusetts there was no one on the primary ballot other than McCarthy; Johnson had decided not to contest the state. As a result, McCarthy picked up the state's entire delegation of seventy-two votes. Similarly, his forces ran well in caucuses in Minnesota and were poised to play a prominent role in that delegation. On March 14 a large turnout of petition signers put McCarthy's name on the primary ballot in California. The morning after the New Hampshire primary Senator McCarthy told the press, "I expect to win in Wisconsin. . . . I think I can get the nomination. I'm ahead now."

McCarthy had no time to savor his good showing in New Hampshire. In exceeding press expectations he changed the nature of the 1968 race among the Democrats. In particular, Senator Robert F. Kennedy now faced a painful choice. During the fall and winter of 1967 he had declined offers to do what McCarthy had done. He had allowed the Minnesota senator to make what seemed to be a feckless race in New Hampshire, and now McCarthy was poised to become the choice among Democratic liberals. While Johnson might still be renominated, at the very least McCarthy was likely to emerge from 1968 as the leader of the party's left wing. Even before New Hampshire the New York senator had been reassessing his refusal to get into the race. As McCarthy's chances improved in New Hampshire, Johnson's electoral vulnerability became more apparent. Kennedy gathered information about entering other primaries and considered what a presidential race might involve. He had to act by March 18 if he wished to enter the delegate-rich California primary.

The week of the New Hampshire primary saw a flurry of negotiations and maneuvers among leading Democrats. On Wednesday, March 13, the day after the vote, Kennedy told reporters he was "actively reconsidering the possibilities that are available to me." That afternoon, in an awkward meeting with McCarthy at the Senate, the two men, who did not like each other, agreed to carry on separate campaigns.

At the same time some Democrats, working on Kennedy's behalf, began looking for a face-saving way for him to make his point without getting into the presidential contest. Mayor Richard Daley of Chicago and former John F. Kennedy aide Theodore Sorensen proposed the idea of a commission of prominent Americans not connected with the administration's Vietnam policy who would review the war situation and make recommendations for future action. Sorensen raised the issue with Johnson on March 11, and after the New Hampshire primary the president asked for a list of those who might serve. Robert Kennedy and Sorensen then met with Clark Clifford, the secretary of defense, on Thursday, March 14, to examine the proposal. The senator said that if the president named individuals who reflected "a clear-cut willingness to seek a wider path to peace in Vietnam," he would not run for president against Johnson. But part of the price for such a declaration would be a statement from the president that his policy in Vietnam "had proved to be in error."

Clifford told the two men that Johnson could not agree to such a statement, and he reminded his visitors that Johnson would probably be nominated, that Johnson could control the foreign policy situation by stopping the bombing or opening negotiations with Hanoi, and that a Kennedy decision to run would guarantee a Republican victory. After Kennedy and Sorensen had left, Clifford laid the idea before Johnson. There was no chance it would be accepted. It would have required Johnson to admit that Robert Kennedy was right and he was wrong, that his Vietnam policy had collapsed, and that he could no longer function fully as president. The commission idea was rejected.

The Kennedy camp also tried to work out an accommodation with McCarthy before the announcement of the New York senator's candidacy. Senator Edward Kennedy flew to Wisconsin to meet with McCarthy to propose a joint anti-Johnson effort. McCarthy showed no interest in such an endeavor, which would have found him carrying the bags of the more charismatic Kennedy. His old animosities against the Kennedys welled up. "That's the way they are," he told his wife Abigail. "When it comes down to it, they never offer anything real."

On Saturday, March 16, Robert Kennedy declared his candidacy for the Democratic presidential nomination in a setting designed to evoke memories of his dead brother's 1960 campaign. The place was the caucus room in the Old Senate Office Building where John Kennedy had announced. The language of the declaration had some of the same intensity: "I do not run for the Presidency merely to oppose any man but to propose new policies." Although he was now running against the expansive foreign policy that his brother had endorsed in 1960, there was some of the same elevated rhetoric. "At stake is not simply the leadership of our party or even our country," Robert Kennedy said, "it is our right to moral leadership on this planet."

Robert Kennedy's death by an assassin's bullet in June 1968 cast a retrospective glow over his last campaign. Viewed more soberly, it is hard to see how he could either have gained the Democratic nomination or have won a general election as his party's choice. In the spring of 1968 there were parts of the country, such as Texas, where he was literally a hated man. He could not enter a sufficient number of primaries to win a majority of the delegates at the national convention. And in the states where he was a likely loser in November, Democratic leaders would not have turned to him against Hubert Humphrey. As was true of the other Democrats who ran for the White House in 1968, Robert Kennedy's personality played as much of a role as political calculation in his decision to seek the presidency. His feud with Lyndon Johnson had to come to a showdown.

The reaction of the McCarthy camp to Kennedy's announced candidacy was predictable outrage at having their man usurped by someone who had been too cautious to run just a few months earlier. One columnist suggested that Kennedy had "come down from the hills to shoot the wounded." The near victory in New Hampshire had changed the McCarthy campaign from a protest candidacy to one that believed in the outside possibility of actually winning the nomination and the presidency. Like Kennedy, Eugene McCarthy had not rationally calculated his chances of accomplishing such a feat. The ability to carry liberal Minnesota in Senate races, to do well in New Hampshire or win a Democratic primary in Wisconsin, did not necessarily translate into a viable national candidacy. In negotiations with him before Kennedy announced, McCarthy had said that he was interested in only one term in the White House as part of "my effort to depersonalize the office" of the president. All Democrats in 1968 seemed to have a sense that whoever won the nomination would have no difficulty at all defeating Richard Nixon or any other

Republican in the autumn. The problem of winning a majority of the electoral vote played little part in the political calculations of leading Democrats during the first six months of 1968.

Johnson reacted to Kennedy's announcement with strident language. Addressing the National Farmers Union on March 18 in Minneapolis, he said of North Vietnam: "We ought not let them win something in Washington that they can't win in Hue, in the I Corps, or in Khe Sanh. And we are not going to." The next day, speaking to a foreign policy conference in Washington, he added, "There is no cheap or no easy way to find the road to freedom and the road to order. But danger and sacrifice built this land and today we are the number one nation. And we are going to stay the number one nation."

The president's bellicose rhetoric struck a discordant note within his own party. His old friend James Rowe told him, "Everyone has turned into a dove." Within the Democratic party sentiment spread toward changing the nation's policy on the war. Moving ahead to increase the military commitment in Vietnam was an unpleasant alternative for many Democrats. "The prospects of a large-scale escalation are threatening to bring down the house," warned a California leader. In Wisconsin, whose primary would be held April 2, the tide was running strongly against the White House. Voters there had concluded, reported the state Democratic chairman, that "within the present context, the war in Vietnam cannot be won, the government of South Vietnam does not enjoy any substantial support from the people, and South Vietnam does not represent a viable political entity worth defending." Without immediate deescalation, the president was told, "this Administration cannot survive politically."

If the perception spread in mid-March 1968 that Lyndon Johnson and his administration sought to pursue their Vietnam policy and to intensify the American commitment, the reality at the White House was quite different. In the aftermath of the Tet offensive, conflicting pressures within the Democratic party and the administration had begun to work a change in the president's policy.

The key figure in the process was the new secretary of defense, Clark Clifford. Later in 1967 Johnson had become disillusioned with Robert S. McNamara, who had been secretary of defense since 1961. After McNamara sent Johnson a November 1 memorandum that outlined his growing doubts about the conduct of the war, the president nominated him to be president of the World Bank. Two months later, on January 18, 1968, Johnson offered Clifford the position of secretary of defense. He made no mention to Clifford of any plans to step down as a presidential candidate. The sixty-one-year-old Clifford came to the cabinet with a reputation as a shrewd political operator gained from service in the Truman administration, to John F. Kennedy, and as a high-priced Washington lawyer. His political instincts were well developed, and he was a clever bureaucratic infighter. He had expressed reservations about the initial escalation of the war in 1965 but from that time forward had supported Johnson's policy. The Senate confirmed Clifford as secretary of defense on January 30, the day the Tet offensive began. The event had a decisive impact on the new cabinet officer. He wrote later: "My faith in our ability to achieve our objectives within an acceptable period of time was shaken and began to erode."

For Clifford and others who had become dubious about continuing the existing policy in Vietnam, a campaign now began to move President Johnson away from further escalation and toward negotiation and a limit to the American commitment in Southeast Asia. During February 1968 the administration discussed various options. From these deliberations came General Westmoreland's request for 206,000 additional troops during 1968. There were military problems with such an increase, but the economic and political implications of the proposal were equally serious. To fund such a further buildup would require a budget increase of up to $12.5 billion during 1968 and 1969. That amount would have devastating effects on inflation and would require new taxes in an election year or the equally unpopular option of wage and price controls. Johnson also feared that funding for his Great Society programs would be endangered if military spending rose. Reaching the troop strength that Westmoreland wanted would mean calling up the reserves and increasing draft calls. Such moves would undoubtedly be politically explosive and could lead to further protests across the nation. Americans would be asked to make new sacrifices for a policy that still could not supply a clear sense of when victory might be reached. One Midwestern politician warned that a call-up of the reserves, for example, would be "political suicide at this time."

The final structure of Johnson's decisions on Vietnam and his own political future evolved during the two weeks after Robert Kennedy entered the presidential race on March 16. The White House had begun to prepare a speech that Johnson would deliver to the country on Sunday, March 31, about his Vietnam policy and future actions in the war. On March 18 Johnson made his hawkish speech in Minnesota. A worried Clifford proposed that the president reconvene a group of senior advisers from outside the government, known as the "Wise Men," to review the situation in Vietnam. They would meet on March 25, six days before the president's speech.

Although Secretary of State Dean Rusk and Clifford were now arguing for a halt in the bombing of most of North Vietnam, Johnson still seemed convinced of the need to continue fighting. He wanted no peace language in the speech. "Let's just make it troops and war," he said to his speech writers. There the matter rested for the next five days. On March 22 Johnson announced that Westmoreland would leave his command in Vietnam to become army chief of staff. Three days later the Wise Men came to the White House.

These fourteen senior statesmen, including former Secretary of State Dean Acheson, Supreme Court Justice Abe Fortas, General Maxwell Taylor, and Arthur Goldberg, ambassador to the United Nations, read documents and heard briefings during their stay. When they met with the president on March 26, McGeorge Bundy, a former assistant to both John F. Kennedy and Johnson, reported the majority's feeling "that we can no longer do the job we set out to do in the time we have left, and we must begin to take steps to disengage." Others disagreed, including Justice Fortas, but the weight of opinion was on the side of limiting the American commitment and pursuing policies to extricate the nation from Vietnam. As Johnson said in his memoirs, if the Wise Men "had been so deeply influenced by the reports of the Tet Offensive, what must the average citizen of the country be thinking?"

By late March 1968 Lyndon Johnson faced a decisive moment in his political career. His position within the Democratic party had further deteriorated since Robert Kennedy had entered the race. Reports from Wisconsin forecast a sizable victory for McCarthy in the April 2 primary. One operative reported, "It's just brutal." When the McCarthy campaign opened a storefront headquarters, "volunteers just pour in. We open one and we're lucky to get two people." On March 28 James Rowe sent Johnson a memorandum titled, "Is the President Running?" Politicians and reporters were deluging him with questions about Johnson's intentions. "This kind of talk has extremely bad effects on the troops in the field," Rowe concluded. The Kennedy forces were saying that the president would not run and that the best course for Democrats was to "Stay loose and stay uncommitted."

The next day the balance shifted. Clifford had suggested that Johnson's speech writer, Harry McPherson, prepare a draft that took a softer line on Vietnam. The draft went to the president late on March 28, and when he went over the speech on Friday, March 29, he used the language from McPherson's "peace" speech. Later that day, as advisers polished the draft, the question arose over a proper ending to the speech. When McPherson proposed to prepare a new conclusion, Johnson told him, "I may have a little ending of my own."

On Saturday, March 30, Johnson called his former speech writer, Horace Busby, who three months earlier had advised the president not to run. Johnson asked him, "What do you think we ought to do?" Busby pointed out that the Wisconsin primary was the following Tuesday, and "it would look bad to quit after a defeat." Johnson asked him to draft a withdrawal statement like the one that had been prepared for the State of the Union message. On Sunday, March 31, there were animated discussions within the Johnson family about the wisdom of the decision, but the president remained firm in his determination to leave politics.

That evening a stunned nation heard Lyndon Johnson first announce that the bombing of North Vietnam would stop except in the area north of the demilitarized zone between North and South Vietnam. He also declared that he was designating Averell Harriman, a veteran diplomat, as his representative to any peace negotiations in which North Vietnam might wish to participate. He stressed American willingness to withdraw if North Vietnam allowed South Vietnam to live in peace. Finally, he reviewed his own public career and then announced, "I shall not seek, and I will not accept the nomination of my party for another term as your President."

The reasons for Lyndon Johnson's withdrawal have been much debated since it was first announced. The initial impulse related to Johnson's uncertain health. His wife had watched his physical condition deteriorate during the early months of 1968. She was an important voice reinforcing his inclination to drop out of politics.

The burdens of the presidency also weighed on Johnson. He found the "goldfish bowl" of the office confining, and by 1967 he was a president almost imprisoned in the White House. Antiwar protesters nagged him at every public engagement, and the safest location for speeches and appearances became military installations. A presidential campaign would have been an ordeal of protest and potential violence no matter how well guarded the chief executive was.

Johnson also knew his political prospects were poor. Aides reassured him that he would win the Democratic nomination and the election. In fact Johnson would have been pressed to gain the nomination and then to run a winning campaign in the fall. His poll ratings showed that more than 52 percent of Americans disliked his policies, and 63 percent were against his handling of the war. His personality and his record would be the focus of Republican attacks. He might win a three-man race against Nixon and George Wallace, but governing the country after the election would be difficult. In a two-man contest with a Republican challenger, Johnson would have little support in the South and West, especially in California. He would also be in serious trouble in the agricultural Midwest. With the Democratic left disaffected, a victorious electoral coalition for Johnson would be difficult to assemble in 1968.

The nature of the battle he faced for the Democratic nomination contributed to Johnson's decision not to run. His hatred of Robert Kennedy was so profound that the prospect of losing the nomination to the New York senator was distasteful in the extreme. He later told a biographer, "The thing I feared from the first day of my Presidency was actually coming true. Robert

Kennedy had openly announced his intention to reclaim the throne in the memory of his brother. And the American people, swayed by the magic of the name, were dancing in the streets. The whole situation was unbearable for me." Rather than face humiliation at Robert Kennedy's hands, Johnson stepped aside and frustrated his rival. The president also eluded a judgment from the American people on the failures of his administration.

The decision followed a familiar pattern in Johnson's life. Before other campaigns he had often wavered about whether he should run. Usually friends or family stiffened his resolve to do what they knew he wanted to do. Lady Bird Johnson had played such a role in 1964 when her husband hesitated before accepting the Democratic nomination. In 1968 no strong voice emerged among the people around Johnson to tell him that he should remain in politics. With their silence they confirmed Johnson's own judgment that his political career was ending.

The president's announcement shook the political landscape in 1968 and realigned the prospects of all the other candidates. The most immediate beneficiary of Johnson's decision seemed to be Robert Kennedy. Richard Nixon said the New York senator should now be favored to win the Democratic nomination. The Kennedy campaign phoned Democrats around the country urging them to enlist with the probable winner. Yet there was no stampede. During the period between his entry into the race and Johnson's withdrawal, Kennedy had waged a frenetic campaign to arouse popular backing for his cause. He had spoken on college campuses to adoring audiences. His themes had been intense. "In the next eight months," he said in Kansas, "we are going to decide what this country will stand for—and what kind of men we are." Since Kennedy lacked the endorsement of Democratic organizations, he had to rely on popular enthusiasm. "I have to win through the people," he said. "Otherwise I am not going to win."

The tone of his speeches and the thrust of his campaign failed to impress the more moderate wing of the Democratic party. Kennedy had been a tough political operator during the 1960 campaign and when he was attorney general. Resentments persisted from his earlier harsh style. The senator could still be abrupt in soliciting support. He called one Democratic woman in the hospital in mid-March and reminded her, "You wouldn't be in Washington if it hadn't been for us." The cumulative impact of Kennedy's emotional public campaign and hardball private tactics left many Democrats still looking for an alternative after Johnson withdrew from the race.

Senator McCarthy won an impressive victory in the Wisconsin primary on April 2. He beat the president easily with 56.2 percent of the vote to Johnson's 34.6 percent. Kennedy received a little more than 6 percent as a write-in candidate. Yet, with Johnson out of the race, the Wisconsin contest seemed an afterthought. McCarthy gained no momentum from his triumph.

Johnson's departure shifted the focus of the McCarthy campaign. He was an attractive protest candidate when the Democratic nominee was likely to be Lyndon Johnson and the chief issue the Vietnam War. With Johnson gone, the question arose of McCarthy's qualifications to be president and his strength as an anti–Robert Kennedy alternative. Even some of his own workers had reservations about McCarthy's capacity to be president. "Every week or two," said a campaign worker, "McCarthy would do or not do something which again brought into question his suitability for the presidency." McCarthy's advocacy of a less powerful chief executive also caused some in his campaign and outside it to wonder whether he could meet the challenges of the office that went beyond the Vietnam War.

There was also the matter of McCarthy's commitment to civil rights. His record in the Senate was generally strong, but he lacked the passionate commitment to the cause that characterized

Robert Kennedy's appeal that spring. Within the McCarthy campaign in Wisconsin, his staff argued about the wisdom of a direct
approach to black voters in Milwaukee. In the end they decided
to add black workers to the campaign team and make McCarthy more visible in ghetto areas. It was not clear how McCarthy
would fare when he had to stand on his own merits against candidates more popular than Johnson.

The president's withdrawal opened the way for still another
Democrat to enter the race. When the year opened, Hubert Humphrey had not expected to have a chance for the White House
in 1968. He anticipated another campaign as Johnson's running
mate. After the events of March 31, however, Humphrey became
the favorite of Democratic moderates and conservatives. He had
learned about the president's decision that Sunday, and Johnson
told him, "If you're going to run, you'd better get ready damn
quick." Humphrey paused only briefly before he concluded that
it was his best remaining chance for the presidency. By the time
he returned to Washington from a trip to Mexico, he was asking
aides, "Has Bobby got it locked up yet?"

The fifty-seven-year-old Humphrey came to the presidential
race with striking credentials and formidable weaknesses. His
strengths grew out of his record as a spokesman for Democratic
liberalism since his 1948 election to the Senate from Minnesota.
On civil rights, health care, and other domestic issues, Humphrey
had been in the vanguard of those who had championed the aspirations of organized labor, the poor, and black Americans. In
foreign policy he had stood for such innovative ideas as the Peace
Corps and limits on nuclear testing. He had been placed on the
ticket in 1964 because his record as a committed liberal would
reassure those with doubts about Johnson's own commitment to
reform.

Humphrey's years as vice president, however, had crippled
his political standing among liberal Democrats. He had been a

loyal subordinate for Johnson, endorsing the policy on Vietnam despite his own doubts about the wisdom of the war. A man of enthusiasms, he had couched his defense of the Vietnam involvement in glowing terms that left many who heard him wondering if the vice president was a sycophant for Johnson. Beyond that question, there were Humphrey's limits as a campaigner. He could be an engrossing public speaker, but his energy often got the best of him and he went on too long. Senators said he could speak a hundred words a minute, with gusts up to two hundred words.

In 1960 Humphrey had run against John F. Kennedy for the nomination. Kennedy's superior political skills and the abundant funds that the Kennedy family poured into the race, as well as some dirty tactics, had defeated him. The loss left its mark. Humphrey wondered now if he had a real chance to win, "or would I just be a punching bag for Kennedy, only to be humiliated and defeated in the Convention?" He had an equally vexing problem with Johnson. He would have to run close to the president's record but somehow establish himself as his own man. "If I run," he told a friend, "Johnson's not going to make it easy." Humphrey's inability to distance himself from the president would plague him throughout 1968.

Humphrey's candidacy faced another formidable obstacle at the outset. Because he was entering the race so late, it would be possible for him to qualify for only two of the spring primaries still to be held. To win the nomination he would have to gather delegates from those states that held caucuses and state conventions. There were more than enough delegates chosen in this way to give Humphrey the nomination; neither Kennedy nor McCarthy could win by running only in the primaries. This route meant, however, that Humphrey would be identified with the older style of Democratic politics and would owe any success to the party leaders and institutions that so many liberal Democrats scorned.

Humphrey really had no choice, but his links with the "old politics" aroused resentments that dogged him until November.

One problem Humphrey did not have during the early weeks of his candidacy was money. As the candidate with the best chance to block Robert Kennedy, he became the beneficiary of all the forces within the Democratic party that sought to head off a Kennedy nomination. Big business, long suspicious of Humphrey's liberalism, now rallied to his campaign. Money from the Johnson presidential effort flowed toward him in April and May. Organized labor also strongly backed Humphrey. Because of Kennedy's attacks on corruption in organized labor during the 1950s and while he was attorney general, many union leaders did not wish to see him in the White House. Humphrey also enjoyed significant support in the South among party leaders. A liberal outsider during the 1950s, he was now the candidate of the Democratic establishment as he pursued the 1,231 delegates he needed for his party's nomination. He announced his candidacy on April 27, 1968. An intense struggle for control of the Democratic party lay ahead.

Johnson's withdrawal also brought about reassessments within Republican ranks. For Richard Nixon, the president's announcement offered him a fortuitous way to keep his Vietnam policy vague and general. Until March 31, pressure had been building on the Republican front-runner to be more specific about his program for Southeast Asia. During March he had indicated that he favored a greater reliance on South Vietnamese troops to bear the brunt of the fighting. Nonetheless he was still less specific about what he would do once in office. His instincts were to remain as quiet as possible on the issue. He told an aide, William Safire, on March 24, "It would be better for me not to do anything controversial for the time being. I don't want to get into the crossfire between LBJ and Bobby—let them hit each other, not me. But I don't like this 'secret plan' business."

For a speech scheduled for March 31, Nixon's aides began drafting a document that advocated a greater use of airpower, less emphasis on "search and destroy" missions aimed at killing the enemy on the ground, and intensified diplomatic pressure on the Soviet Union and China to bring about a negotiated settlement of the Vietnam War. In effect, Nixon reached the same conclusion as the Johnson administration: winning the war in Vietnam was not possible within the limits of the resources available to the United States. But Nixon did not have to set out his conclusions on March 31. When the White House asked the networks for time to carry the president's speech, Nixon canceled his address.

The day after the president's withdrawal announcement, Nixon declared that he would make no further public statements about Vietnam and the war for several weeks while the president was conducting his negotiations. In effect, the Republican leader could now avoid saying anything specific about his intentions. He also began a tacit political alliance with Lyndon Johnson that persisted throughout much of 1968 and had a significant effect on the outcome of the election.

By March 31 Nixon had also apparently staved off a challenge from his most serious Republican rival. After Nixon won in New Hampshire, moderate Republicans pressed Nelson Rockefeller to enter the race. Rockefeller very much wanted to be president. Governor of New York since 1959, he believed his talents suited him for the White House. His race against Barry Goldwater in 1964, however, had left conservative Republicans embittered against him. Rockefeller always looked better as a potential presidential candidate than he did once he formally announced. He preferred to be selected rather than have to pursue the nomination. In early 1968 his soundings indicated that he would not succeed against Nixon. Rockefeller thus announced on March 21 that he would not be a candidate in 1968. In the process the New York governor embarrassed a key supporter. Governor Spiro Agnew of Maryland had organized a Draft Rockefeller Committee, and the announcement took him by surprise. Nixon soon made personal overtures to Agnew, and the two men found a common rapport that grew as the national convention neared.

The Republican nomination thus seemed to be safely in Nixon's grasp by April 1, 1968. He knew, however, that his real opposition might come from Ronald Reagan on the right of the party. The California governor was preserving his pose of non-candidacy while he waited to see if Nixon might falter. Reagan was already an effective fund-raiser for party candidates, and he continued to be a drawing card on the Republican banquet circuit. Reagan's strategy was to be a favorite-son candidate from California, block Nixon's nomination on the first ballot, and thus inherit his Southern and Western support. But first Nixon would have to be stopped, and that eventuality seemed less and less probable as the spring of 1968 progressed.

Meanwhile George Wallace was having growing success in placing his name on the ballot in every state. His standing in the polls showed a slow but perceptible rise. In one poll in October 1967 he was the choice of 10 percent of the voters. By March 1968 he had climbed to 15 percent of the vote in a three-way contest with Nixon and Johnson. One pollster concluded a few months later that "the strong possibility exists that third-party candidate George Wallace would deny either major party candidate the electoral votes needed to win."

Between the time of the Tet offensive and Johnson's departure from the presidential race, the issue of Vietnam dominated the public agenda. To that extent the election came to seem that it was about the American role in Southeast Asia rather than any domestic issue. The impression was misleading. Events following the speech of Lyndon Johnson on March 31 demonstrated the extent to which other issues were animating the electorate. On April 4, 1968, Dr. Martin Luther King, Jr., was assassinated in Memphis, Tennessee. Across the nation blacks expressed their grief and anger in demonstrations and riots. The issue of race and the problem of "law and order" forced its way back into the presidential election of 1968. American society faced a time of turmoil and testing over an unpopular war and the question of racial justice.

3

The Violent Spring

DURING 1968 the nation seemed to lurch from one shock to another. Four days after Lyndon Johnson's political abdication and two days after Eugene McCarthy won the Wisconsin primary, Dr. Martin Luther King, Jr., was killed at the Lorraine Motel where he was staying in Memphis, Tennessee. He was in Memphis to lend support to a strike of garbage workers. Reports of his assassination provoked rage and violence among blacks across the nation. In Washington, D.C., New York, Chicago, and other cities large and small, arson, rioting, and looting erupted during the days that followed. "This is it, baby," said one black man in Washington. "The shit is going to hit the fan now. We ought to burn the place down right now." Ten people died in Washington, and more than seven hundred fires were set.

Politicians had focused on the war in Vietnam as the nation's major concern during the first three months of 1968. In a larger sense, the issue of race was a more salient domestic problem for Americans black and white at the end of the 1960s. The civil rights revolution, and the response that followed it, revealed tensions within the body politic over this most volatile of subjects. King's death laid bare the extent to which race still divided Americans during the presidency of Lyndon Johnson.

By 1968 the idealistic fervor for civil rights evident at the beginning of the decade had greatly diminished. An issue that had helped Democrats with the voters through 1964 now became an electoral liability. Fissures between blacks and whites had widened. In addition, African Americans themselves quarreled about how best to pursue their agenda. For many blacks the achievements of the civil rights movement had not brought them close to economic or social equality with whites.

Initially the civil rights campaigns of the early 1960s had commanded the support of most white Americans outside the South. In February 1964, for example, 72 percent of non-Southern whites told the Gallup poll that the Johnson administration was "about right" or was not "fast enough" in its push for civil rights. The Civil Rights Act of 1964, which established legal equality in public accommodations and outlawed segregation in education and employment, and the Voting Rights Act of 1965, which struck down political barriers to black participation, seemed evenhanded efforts to assure all citizens equal treatment under the law. For most Northern voters, segregation was at bottom a Southern problem. They did not expect that extending these legal rights to blacks would change the way race relations functioned outside of Dixie.

But problems arose after 1965 when the federal government enforced these new statutes. Carrying the provisions of the law into practice demanded bureaucratic decrees from Washington that addressed segregated school systems, discrimination in housing and employment, and the allocation of tax revenues. As these issues and policies moved outside the South to affect Northern voters in middle-class and lower-middle-class areas, support for the Democratic civil rights program dropped. Voters saw it as a threat to property values, neighborhood integrity, and ethnic cohesion. As a labor union official wrote after Democratic defeats in the 1966 elections, "All over the country, civil rights is now equated with losing the savings invested in your home."

Equally devastating to Democrats was the emergence of urban violence as a black response to conditions in the nation's large cities. The 1965 riots in the Watts district of Los Angeles were not the first such disturbances. During 1964 there had been outbreaks of rioting in New York, Philadelphia, and Paterson, New Jersey. The Watts violence received extensive television coverage of black youths engaged in looting and random destruction. Coming within days of the passage of the 1965 Voting Rights Act, the Watts riots indicated that legislation alone could not solve the racial issue.

During the "long, hot summers" of 1966, 1967, and 1968, ghetto riots became a fixture in the United States. Democrats faced the problem of explaining how their programs to deal with black grievances had evoked such a destructive response. Republicans charged that the Johnson administration was undermining social stability. "We have been talking a long time about color," said Senator Everett M. Dirksen, the Republican leader in the Senate, "when in fact we should also be talking about conduct." By August 1966 the Harris poll found that 70 percent of white Americans now believed that blacks were "trying to move too fast."

As white sentiment toward civil rights cooled, opinion among blacks was moving in a contrasting direction. The emphasis had shifted from a demand for legal equality to a more assertive call for equal economic and social conditions. A militant mood had appeared, especially among younger blacks who did not wish to wait for white America to grant them rights and privileges that should have been theirs all along. In the North such leaders as Stokely Carmichael of the Student Nonviolent Coordinating Committee had galvanized his audiences with strong language. "We have been saying freedom for six years—and we ain't got

nothin'. What we are gonna start saying now is 'Black Power.'"
The black civil rights movement broke apart over the issue of
Black Power. Those who believed in the need for coalitions with
whites confronted those, such as Carmichael, who urged blacks
to use their own resources in the struggle.

The most visible victim of this process was Martin Luther
King. He had become a national figure during the 1950s when
he first led the boycott of blacks against the system of segregated
buses in Montgomery, Alabama. King preached a gospel of non-
violence based on the teachings of Henry David Thoreau and
Mohandas Gandhi. Soon he was the apparent embodiment of the
civil rights struggle and its most eloquent champion. His speech
during the March on Washington, with its moving cadences of "I
have a dream," touched the national conscience. His demonstrations in Selma, Alabama, and elsewhere laid the groundwork for
passage of the Civil Rights Act of 1964 and the Voting Rights
Act of 1965. To many whites King seemed a responsible black
spokesman working for constructive policies.

As other blacks moved to a more militant position, King experienced the more subtle racism of the North in campaigns to
integrate housing in Chicago. He also became critical of the war
in Vietnam. "In a real sense," he said in April 1967, "the Great
Society has been shot down on the battlefields of Vietnam."
King's attack on Johnson's war policies separated him from the
White House. He moved closer to embracing socialism as a way
to redistribute the wealth of the nation. He promised to unite
the peace movement and the civil rights movement "until the
very foundations of our nation are shaken." No matter what King
did, he could not satisfy young blacks who wanted a revolution
in the United States, but his language angered the administration and mainstream black leaders who had access to politicians
and power. By the time Johnson withdrew from the presidential race, King's career was in crisis. A few weeks before he was

murdered, he was discussing more aggressive tactics of nonvio-
lence and social disruption to end the war and achieve rights for
black Americans.

The riots that broke out when King was killed soon led
to congressional action on an open-housing bill that had been
stalled in Congress. Republicans supported the bill in part to
avoid a stronger law and, at Richard Nixon's request, to remove
the issue from the forthcoming campaign. The law represented
a symbolic response of white America to what had happened in
the wake of King's death. The other reaction of whites, however,
was more ominous in both political and social terms. Chicago's
mayor Richard J. Daley had ordered his police to "shoot to kill"
rioters in that city. Political candidates soon began to emphasize
law-and-order appeals in their speeches. Richard Nixon took
readily to such a theme, and in his campaign appearances during
the spring he declared, to appreciative applause, "Some of our
courts have gone too far in weakening the police forces as against
the criminal forces, and we must restore the balance."

Nixon framed his appeals for law and order in language that
prevented opponents from accusing him of racial demagoguery.
Such considerations did not trouble the candidate outside the existing party system, whose ability to tap the racial fears of white
Americans was making him a significant element in presidential
politics, George C. Wallace of Alabama.

Wallace told a Washington press conference on February 8,
1968, that he intended to enter the presidential race. "The bureaucrats and rhetoricians in Washington" should let "people in
Ohio and New York and California decide themselves . . . what
type of school system they are going to have," said Wallace's campaign literature. Politicians and reporters time and again under-
rated Wallace's prospects as his candidacy got rolling. Democrats
preferred not to face the implications of his appeal to Northern
white voters. Republicans were just as anxious to avoid consider-

ing what Wallace did to the GOP's growing allure for Southern whites. With Wallace in a three-candidate race, Republicans and Democrats were deadlocked. Polls indicated that Wallace would win about 10 percent of the vote in such a contest, and during the spring of 1968 his total was creeping up.

By the time he went out on the campaign trail, the feisty Wallace had become adept at tapping into the resentment that his supporters felt about the direction in which society was moving. He made no outright racist appeals. "I am not against anybody because of color," he said. "I never have been." Instead he charged, "The Communist movement has been behind the civil rights movement." When he said that "it was never intended for the Federal Government to run the policies of local schools," his cheering audiences knew he was talking about desegregation and civil rights. "Integration is a matter to be decided by each State," he contended. "The States must determine if they feel it is of benefit to both races."

Wallace delivered these messages with practiced skill. His rallies had the flavor of a Country and Western stage show, a religious revival, and a political camp meeting. His standard lines drew thunderous applause. If he faced demonstrators as president, he knew how he would deal with them. "When we get to be President, and some anarchist lies down in front of our car, it'll be the *last* car he'll ever lie down in front of." He tried to find the common bond of resentment among white voters North and South. "People always say that George Wallace just appeals to the crackers, the peckerwoods, and the rednecks," Wallace would say. As the crowd waited for the punch line, he added, "Well, George Wallace says there's an awful lot of us rednecks in this country—*and they're not all in the South!*" When he denounced liberals and bureaucrats, his listeners shouted their agreement.

The formal announcement of Wallace's candidacy came on April 1. His campaign was well financed, and his organization had placed his name on the ballot in all fifty states. Knowing he could not be elected president himself, Wallace hoped to hold the balance of power in a deadlocked election. He "would have the power to say just who *would* be the next President. And I make no secret that I would want something in return before I make my choice."

The social resentments that propelled Wallace to national prominence formed the context for the campaigns of the major party candidates during the spring of 1968. For Richard Nixon, Wallace posed a clear threat to his electoral chances once Nixon had received the Republican nomination. In April, little disturbed the smooth progress of the Nixon campaign. He easily defeated Ronald Reagan in the Wisconsin primary, where the California governor's name was on the ballot but he did not campaign. As the month ended, however, reports circulated that Nelson Rockefeller was reconsidering his earlier decision not to seek the presidency.

Urged on by Lyndon Johnson in secret and in public by major business leaders, Rockefeller announced on April 30 that he was back in the race. Since it was unlikely he could defeat Nixon in Republican primaries, Rockefeller needed to show he was electable where Nixon, a two-time loser, was not. Then the victory-hungry Republicans would abandon Nixon for a proven winner. It was an ill-conceived approach. Rank-and-file Republicans across the nation hated Rockefeller as a man who had opposed Barry Goldwater in 1964, symbolized big government in New York State, and was trying to buy the GOP nomination. Even if the poll results ran Rockefeller's way, many Republicans would never turn to his candidacy. "If the polls show you well ahead of Nixon, that's going to make you even less popular" with Republicans, an aide told Rockefeller.

The New Yorker spent a great deal of money during May and June, won the Massachusetts primary on the day he announced, and saw the polls move in his favor to a marginal degree. Surveys did not show, however, that Nixon would lose in the fall. In fact, in the Indiana, Nebraska, and Oregon primaries Nixon won striking victories over both Rockefeller and Reagan when their names appeared on the ballot. The average Republican wanted Nixon as his party's presidential candidate more than Rockefeller. Whether Republicans would feel the same way in a Reagan-Nixon confrontation remained to be seen. For the moment, Rockefeller's entry into the Republican race had fallen flat. As June began, his candidacy was lifeless.

Nixon continued to build his campaign appeal on the basis of voter uneasiness with the way the nation was moving on domestic issues. He tried out themes that would serve him well in the fall and would become lasting features of Republican campaigns into the future. What the country needed, he said on May 16, was a "new alignment for American unity" which would produce "a significant breakthrough toward what America needs: peaceful, orderly progress." For the first time he began talking about "the silent center, the millions of people in the middle of the political spectrum who do not demonstrate, who do not picket or protest loudly." His campaign literature proclaimed that "there is no cause that justifies rule by mob instead of by reason." He found in the nation "a rebellion against taxes, and against the ever-higher piling of Federal tax on state tax on local tax."

Wooing the South for its electoral votes and to stave off any challenge from Reagan, Nixon courted Senator John Tower of Texas and Senator Strom Thurmond of South Carolina. Thurmond was especially central to Nixon's chances; he had been the candidate of the State's Rights party in 1948 and was "the only Southern leader in the GOP who could rally Southerners to a Republican banner." At a meeting in Atlanta on May 31, Nixon assured Thurmond and other Southern Republicans that he would name conservatives to the Supreme Court, oppose "busing as a means of achieving racial balance in schools," and increase defense spending. The defense issue was particularly important to Thurmond whose state had several key military installations. The South Carolina senator announced his support for Nixon a few days later when he said that the Republican front-runner "offers the best hope of recovering from domestic lawlessness, a bloody no-win war in Southeast Asia; runaway spending and rising costs of living; strategic military inferiority; loss of influence in world affairs; and a power-grasping Supreme Court." Thurmond would prove to be the key to Nixon's convention success with Southern delegates.

While Republicans remained relatively unified during the spring, and Nixon's bandwagon rolled along without serious public opposition, the Democrats encountered bitter factionalism after Johnson's withdrawal and the murder of Martin Luther King, Jr. Each one of the major candidates—Kennedy, McCarthy, and Humphrey—pursued the nomination during April and May. In the process, whatever remained of party unity vanished in a series of acrimonious primary and convention battles. Personality clashes and ideological disputes overshadowed electoral considerations and any kind of rational judgment about what was needed to beat the Republicans in the fall campaign. Still believing they were the normal majority party, Democrats failed to adjust to the presence of a competitive Republican party and the third-party challenge of George Wallace.

In the wake of Johnson's withdrawal, the conventional wisdom in the press was that Robert Kennedy had become the front-runner for the nomination. Such a judgment rested on a faith in the Kennedy mystique among the American people and the presumed efficiency of the Kennedy organization. It took less account of Kennedy's specific problems as a national candidate for president. Despite his celebrity status, the New York senator was not as formidable in electoral terms as people at the time and later historians have believed. In May 1968, for example, he trailed Nixon by ten percentage points in the polls.

In any case, neither Eugene McCarthy nor Hubert Humphrey was prepared to step aside and concede the Democratic nomination to Robert Kennedy. McCarthy told aides, "It's narrowed down to Bobby and me." He intended to make Kennedy campaign against his own legacy. "We'll make him run against Jack . . . and I'm Jack." In the absence of Lyndon Johnson, however, McCarthy's campaign lacked a clear public rationale. His supporters were a diverse mixture of radical Democrats who found even Robert Kennedy too conservative for their tastes, and liberals who looked back longingly to the articulate messages of Adlai Stevenson. For black and working-class audiences, McCarthy still had little to offer. He seemed out of step with the black and Hispanic Democrats with whom Kennedy naturally communicated.

McCarthy's campaign reflected the ambivalence of its candidate. It was poorly organized, and McCarthy was not disposed to give his workers clear direction and purpose. "He seemed to pay no attention at all to his campaign," recalled one operative. "He viewed it as a spontaneous happening which he should not try to control." The presidential candidate was easily distracted, disliked emotional appeals and sometimes seemed above all the excitement of the campaign. Some Democrats responded to his cool aloofness, others found his detachment infuriating. In the spring of 1968 his sudden rise to prominence gave him an untested electoral appeal that made him a difficult opponent for both Kennedy and Hubert Humphrey.

After rallying endorsements from party regulars during April and lining up funds to sustain his campaign, Vice President Humphrey prepared to announce his candidacy on April 27. In terms of national electoral appeal, he was the strongest of the three Democratic hopefuls in 1968. As northern liberals, Kennedy, McCarthy, and Humphrey all had limited support in the South and border states. Except for the Pacific Coast, they were also weak in the West. McCarthy ran well in the suburbs but not in the inner cities. Kennedy could capture the black voters in the cities and some of the disaffected white ethnic voters. Humphrey had residual strength in each of these constituencies. One key to Humphrey's strength with party regulars was their sense that he would do the least electoral damage to local Democrats in the fall.

Humphrey approached his announcement with typical ebullience. "Here we are," he told his audience, "the way politics ought to be in America, the politics of happiness, the politics of purpose, the politics of joy. And that's the way it's going to be all the way, from here on in." The phrase "the politics of joy" struck a discordant note among liberals who regarded it as further evidence of how out of touch with events Humphrey had become as part of the Johnson administration. Nonetheless Humphrey achieved good results in states where he needed to do well. During late April and into May he won a strong majority of delegates in such states as Maryland and Pennsylvania. Humphrey headquarters predicted he would be nominated on the first ballot; polls indicated he was the choice among rank-and-file Democratic voters.

Humphrey's lead emerged despite problems with his campaign organization. To appeal to the younger voters who seemed so crucial in 1968, he named Senators Fred Harris of Oklahoma and Walter Mondale of Minnesota to run his canvass, United Democrats for Humphrey. A number of people played important roles, including his vice-presidential aides, old political friends from Minnesota, and longtime Democratic allies. The result was an organization of confused and shifting alignments which confirmed the Washington perception that Humphrey was not a good administrator. Still, the candidate's main problem remained his relationship with Lyndon Johnson and Humphrey's need to establish his own political identity.

While Humphrey moved toward a nomination based on delegates obtained in the convention states, between early May and early June McCarthy and Kennedy waged a series of bitter primary battles in Indiana, Nebraska, Oregon, and California. The press concentrated on this exciting horse race between two famous Democrats to see who would become the most credible alternative to the vice president. Democratic liberalism indulged in a fratricidal display which further contributed to the electoral problems of the party in 1968 and beyond.

The McCarthy-Kennedy struggle occurred as American society watched with dismay further examples of upheaval among the younger generation on college campuses. The most famous and visible of these confrontations occurred at Columbia University in New York City. Located on Morningside Heights above the black district of Harlem, Columbia had long had a tense relationship with its neighbors. In 1968 these pressures focused on the university's plans to construct a new gymnasium in Morningside Park. While part of the proposed facility would be available for the use of local residents, most of the gym would serve the predominantly white and affluent student body of Columbia. At a time when students nationally were protesting the insensitivity of research universities to social needs and their willingness to collaborate with the established order, the Columbia gym issue aroused animosities among the university's small black population. Radical students at Columbia distrusted the university's position on the draft and were looking for an occasion to dramatize their grievances. The gym issue thus served as an excuse for radical Columbia students to publicize their marginal position within higher education.

Protests against the gymnasium and the Vietnam War at Columbia on April 23, 1968, led to a student occupation of the main

building at the university. Within a few days five more build-
ings were seized. The students demanded that the gymnasium
not be built and that the university recognize the Vietnam War
was wrong. They also wanted amnesty for their actions. Negotiations failed to produce a settlement. Instead, on April 30 the
New York City police evicted the occupying students. More than
500 students were arrested and 148 people injured, including
20 police. Three weeks later another occupation occurred, with
another equally violent confrontation. This time more than 175
people were arrested and 68 were injured.

The events on Morningside Heights were another indication
to American voters of a rapidly unraveling social fabric. Turmoil
on campuses, like urban rioting, aroused fears about the stability
of law and order in the nation. Richard Nixon called the events
at Columbia "the first major skirmish in a revolutionary struggle
to seize the universities of this country and transform them into
sanctuaries for radicals and vehicles for revolutionary politics
and social goals." Since the language of the Columbia protesters
resembled what Democratic contenders were saying on the campaign trail—about the Vietnam War, racism, and the failure of
the older generation, for example—voters blamed the party for
fostering campus unrest.

The confrontation between Eugene McCarthy and Robert Kennedy began with the Indiana primary on May 7. It was
not a state likely to be carried by any Democratic candidate in
1968. Indiana had voted for the Democratic presidential choice
only twice, in 1936 and 1964, and Nixon was favored to win
easily in the general election. Wallace sentiment was strong in
the southern part of the state, and racial tensions were evident
in the industrialized north with its substantial black population.
The Democratic party organization, led by Governor Roger D.
Branigan, was hostile to both liberal candidates, especially Ken-

nedy. The Democratic primary became a three-way race, with Branigan as the favorite-son candidate of the regulars who had supported Johnson and now preferred Humphrey. Still, Kennedy and his aides decided that Indiana offered the best opportunity to knock McCarthy out of the race quickly and make the search for delegates a choice between Humphrey and Kennedy. When Kennedy went in, McCarthy did so as well.

Kennedy and his family poured several million dollars into the primary, blanketing the state with radio and television commercials, billboards, and literature. The goal was to assemble a coalition of the state's black voters and white ethnic working-class Democrats who had admired John Kennedy. In the highly conservative climate of Indiana during the spring of 1968, Senator Edward Kennedy later recalled in his 2009 memoir, "we found that Indianans didn't necessarily like Bobby's 'super-hot' style." Accordingly, Robert Kennedy emphasized more than he had in the past his law-and-order credentials as a former attorney general who had been "for three-and-half years, chief law enforcement officer of the United States." He cut his hair, muted his speaking style, and played down his similarities to his late brother. These changes sought to soften Kennedy's perceived image as "a too-aggressive opportunist running on John Kennedy's reputation, with too much of an appeal to the very young and immature."

In Indiana, where anti-war protests were unpopular, Kennedy changed his stance on the Vietnam War. Placing less emphasis on a negotiated settlement of the conflict, he argued for improving U.S. military and diplomatic prospects. On domestic issues he talked of the role businessmen could play in addressing the problems of the cities, including tax credits for firms that helped develop the inner city. These statements were necessary concessions to conservative sentiments in Indiana, but they

illustrated Democratic problems in 1968 in appealing to the
broad electorate. Republicans could always make a stronger case
for the same policies.

Eugene McCarthy's campaign did not go well in Indiana.
Johnson's withdrawal had left McCarthy's student canvassers
without the war issue to emphasize to the voters. As a result, the
impact of young people was not as effective as it had been in New
Hampshire. Within the campaign organization itself, discord
prevailed as local McCarthy supporters quarreled with members
of his national leadership. There were mixups in speaking sched-
ules; campaign literature was not available; and the focus of the
canvass was on sparsely populated rural Indiana. "At times we
were ready to shoot ourselves," said one McCarthy worker.

McCarthy's residual appeal remained intact. For Democrats
who disliked Johnson and Kennedy in equal measure, the senator from Minnesota seemed a calm, rational alternative. The enthusiastic crowds that surrounded Kennedy made other voters
fearful. McCarthy played on these apprehensions with his calls
for "your patience, your attention" as he offered "a politics of
participation and a politics of personal response on the part of the
citizens of this country." There was also a good deal of innovation in some of McCarthy's themes. "The Cold War in Europe
is over," he argued. "There's no need to go on fighting it." As he
had before, he called for the ouster of J. Edgar Hoover, director
of the Federal Bureau of Investigation, and the replacement of
Secretary of State Dean Rusk, one of the more hawkish members
of Johnson's cabinet. Attacks on these established figures pleased
McCarthy's liberal fans but did little to reassure Indiana voters
about the candidate's concern for the economic and social issues
of inflation and crime.

When the votes were tallied on May 7, Kennedy led the
field in Indiana. He received 42.3 percent of the total, or 328,118
votes, to Branigan's 30.7 percent and McCarthy's 27 percent

(209,965 votes). The outcome satisfied neither McCarthy nor Kennedy. For Kennedy the victory was not so decisive that it would drive McCarthy from the field. In fact, since McCarthy had done slightly better than expected, the Minnesota senator believed the primary was a positive for him. "We have tested the enemy," he said. "We know his techniques, we know his weaknesses."

Kennedy won the black vote easily but also did well in blue-collar districts where Wallace had shown strength. From these facts observers at the time and scholars since have concluded that Kennedy's showing in Indiana indicated he might be able to achieve a working coalition of whites and blacks and heal some of the rifts among Democrats. That conclusion exaggerates the significance of Kennedy's Indiana vote. In the Republican primary, Nixon polled 508,000 votes, more than any one of the Democratic contenders, and he won more than a million votes when he carried the state against Humphrey and Wallace in the fall. Kennedy's coalition represented more the hard core of the Democratic base in Indiana than a potential nucleus of a winning majority in the general election.

While Kennedy and McCarthy fought in Indiana, Humphrey continued to amass convention delegates with regularity. His confident managers, Senators Mondale and Harris, talked of a first-ballot victory. Meanwhile the primary race moved on to the Western plains in the Nebraska election of May 14. From the outset, the McCarthy effort in Nebraska was minimal. The main emphasis of his campaign was directed toward the next primary in the friendlier state of Oregon, and the resources committed to Nebraska were limited. For Kennedy, on the other hand, Nebraska was an attractive race. The farm policies of the Johnson administration were unpopular with Nebraska Democrats, and Kennedy began the race with a double-digit lead over McCarthy in the polls.

Nebraska was a strongly Republican state which had voted overwhelmingly for Nixon against John Kennedy in 1960. Fewer than 200,000 Democratic voters had to be reached, and the Kennedy organization could use its resources for phone banks and campaign workers to blanket the state. While Kennedy's appearances in Nebraska were successful, McCarthy seemed uninterested and more focused on Oregon. The result was a striking Kennedy victory on May 14. He won almost 52 percent of the vote to McCarthy's 32 percent. The Kennedy forces immediately sought to dismiss McCarthy as a serious alternative to their man. He was, said one Kennedy aide, no longer "a credible candidate."

Such talk did not impress McCarthy, who sensed that Oregon would be friendlier territory for the kind of campaign he was making. "We are going on to Oregon," he told supporters after the Nebraska vote. The Oregon primary, held a week before the California contest, would be a significant test going into the most important primary of the year in the Golden State. The result in Nebraska indicated that Kennedy appealed to the base of Democratic support, as he had shown in Indiana. But there was little chance he or any Democrat could carry Nebraska in the fall. Nixon won the state by a wide margin six months later.

McCarthy's campaign, battered after two consecutive primary defeats, revived in the more favorable atmosphere of Oregon. Long opposed to the Vietnam War, Democrats in the state cheered McCarthy's early denunciations of the Asian conflict. In a state with few minorities and a relative absence of serious urban problems, Kennedy's concern with the nation's social ills seemed irrelevant. Organized labor disliked Kennedy because of his role in opposing the Teamsters union in the 1950s. For McCarthy the rural state with small towns and cities was well suited to his low-key rhetoric and Minnesota farm background. The McCarthy workers in Oregon were well organized, and in this instance the Kennedy campaign suffered because of its dependence on the help of Representative Edith Green. (The Kennedy campaign believed her to be more powerful than she really was.) Early polls showed McCarthy running even with Kennedy. A sizable pro-Johnson vote remained among party conservatives, and it was likely to turn to McCarthy in the polling booths. During a speech in California in mid-May, Kennedy said, "I think that if I get beaten in any primary, I am not a very viable candidate." His comment raised the stakes of the Oregon primary.

By the time of the Oregon race, tensions between Kennedy and McCarthy had intensified. During earlier races, supporters of Kennedy had circulated leaflets attacking McCarthy for his Senate votes against a minimum-wage law in 1960 and against a provision of the 1965 Voting Rights Act to repeal the poll tax in the South. McCarthy's camp responded with charges that Kennedy had engaged in illegal wiretapping during his service as attorney general, including the telephone of Martin Luther King, Jr. These nasty exchanges probably influenced few Democratic voters. As Kennedy conceded, the people who voted for McCarthy would have done so even if he had voted wrong on issues consistently. They were that bitter. The emotional temperature of the strife among Democrats was rising, reducing the changes for reestablishing party unity for the general election.

In Oregon McCarthy sharpened his attacks on the Vietnam War and the links between war policies that spanned the Kennedy and Johnson administrations. That approach hit Robert Kennedy at a vulnerable point, for the New York senator was now attacking policies with which his dead brother had been identified. "Involvement in Vietnam was no accident," said McCarthy, "it did not happen overnight." There was continuity in how Americans had conducted their foreign affairs, McCarthy charged, for which Robert Kennedy needed to answer. "Any man who played a prominent role in developing the policies of the early sixties, I think, can be called upon to explain his role in those policies, and not just in those policies but in the development of the process." McCarthy indicated he would not under any circumstances reach an accommodation with Kennedy.

Robert Kennedy never found his stride in Oregon. His high-intensity campaigning style put voters off, as it had done in Indiana. As defeat neared, his heightened efforts compounded his problems. An aide observed that Oregon "is all one great white middle-class suburb" whose voters Kennedy "frightened." With the United States moving toward a politics in which these suburbs would hold increasing electoral power, Kennedy's difficulties in Oregon suggest that his national coalition-building powers had inherent limits.

McCarthy defeated Kennedy in Oregon on May 28. The Minnesota senator received 45 percent of the vote to 39 percent for Kennedy; the remainder was scattered among Johnson, Humphrey, and write-in ballots. At the McCarthy victory celebration, the crowd chanted, "Gene in '68, Bobby'll have to wait." McCarthy told them, "Here we had the right issues and the right candidate, and here it was just a question of finding our constituency." Kennedy congratulated McCarthy and accepted his family's first electoral defeat with public grace. But as it turned out, the Oregon results did not help McCarthy. Kennedy's defeat boosted Humphrey's chances for the nomination and thus worked against McCarthy's long-range aspirations for the presidency. And the bitterness now generated between the McCarthy and Kennedy camps proved an important element in the continuing factional warfare that plagued the Democrats throughout 1968.

Kennedy's chances for the nomination now hinged on victory in California. If he failed to win that large bloc of delegates, he would have no chance to convince wavering Democrats in the East to leave Humphrey and support his candidacy. Should he lose in California, the delegates already committed to him would jump on the Humphrey bandwagon overnight. McCarthy, for his part, needed a win over Kennedy to emerge as the anti-Humphrey alternative—though some of his staff members thought a narrow loss would be best. Such a result would keep Kennedy and Mc-Carthy evenly balanced as opponents of Humphrey and increase the possibility of a deadlocked national convention. In either event, McCarthy had to campaign with vigor in California if he wished to make a respectable showing against Kennedy.

In terms of organization and money, the primary contest in California was now one of relative equals. The long-standing anti-war sentiment in the state provided the grassroots base for the McCarthy campaign. His triumph in Oregon brought in fresh contributions which enabled his campaign to purchase the huge amounts of television and radio advertising needed to cover California's large population. The candidate himself was more involved in the race than in the earlier primaries, and that added energy to his canvass in California between May 29 and June 4.

Kennedy's campaign was equally well organized and effi-cient, with a network of one hundred local headquarters across the state, an abundance of volunteers, and ample funds for me-dia messages. The candidate's most secure base was among black and Hispanic voters. Kennedy appeared in minority precincts to intense public adoration. Tens of thousands of people would surge toward his car, trying to touch him or shake his hand. Among white voters in the California suburbs, however, senti-ment was split between Kennedy and McCarthy. The Minnesota lawmaker ran well among Democrats who had voted for Adlai Stevenson during the 1950s.

Until California, Kennedy had refused to stage a public de-bate with McCarthy. After the Oregon result, Kennedy could no longer use his perceived front-runner status to avoid a con-frontation with his rival. The two men appeared on a television broadcast on June 1 for their first face-to-face encounter of the campaign. Neither prepared diligently for the debate. The Mc-Carthy camp was confident its man would easily win; Kennedy held briefings but seemed distracted.

The debate itself had some heated moments. When asked what they would do about Vietnam, McCarthy indicated that a coalition government, including some Communists, was necessary to bring the war to an end. Kennedy challenged that position because it would involve "forcing a coalition on the government of Saigon." As he had done in Indiana, Kennedy was careful not to repudiate the war. McCarthy responded that he would accept such a coalition but would not impose it on South Vietnam.

In a key exchange on the issue of the cities and the problems of race, Kennedy suggested that the government invest in the rehabilitation of ghetto areas. It would be better, McCarthy offered, to relocate some ghetto residents in areas outside the inner city. Kennedy replied that such a strategy might produce "catastrophic" results, and he added the inflammatory remark, "You say you are going to take ten thousand black people and move them into Orange County" (a conservative suburb near Los Angeles). There were further discussions of Kennedy's responsibility for the policies and failures of his brother's administration.

Going into the debate the conventional wisdom had been that McCarthy was the superior performer who would handle the less adept Kennedy. When the two men battled on even terms for most of the program, Kennedy exceeded the press's expectations. In the reaction to the debate, newspaper polls put Kennedy ahead of his rival. "It was clear," said one McCarthy speech writer, "that Kennedy could take McCarthy head-on with no fear of his magic powers." Whether it was boredom on McCarthy's part or a fear of showing more eagerness for the nomination than he believed a candidate should, McCarthy missed a chance to establish an evident superiority over his rival. The debate took much of the steam out of McCarthy's campaign workers.

The results on June 4 gave Kennedy a victory in the California primary—clear, but not as decisive as his supporters had hoped for. He gathered 46.4 percent of the vote to 41.8 percent for McCarthy. A slate of former Johnson supporters won about 12 percent. At the same time Kennedy won a strong success in the South Dakota primary, where he had 50 percent of the vote to 20 percent for McCarthy. Delegates pledged to Johnson and Hubert Humphrey gained 30 percent of the vote in the state. That election night Kennedy hoped he might now persuade the McCarthy supporters "that I'm the only candidate against the war that can beat Humphrey." He added, "My only chance is to chase Hubert's ass all over the country."

Robert Kennedy, of course, never got the chance to implement that strategy. He made a victory statement in the Embassy Ballroom at the Ambassador Hotel in Los Angeles shortly after midnight on June 5, 1968. He pledged to heal the divisions within the country, "whether it's between blacks and whites, between the poor and the more affluent, or between age groups or on the war in Vietnam," so that the nation "can start to work together." Leaving the ballroom, he was passing through a hotel kitchen when he was fatally wounded by an assassin, Sirhan Sirhan. Robert Kennedy died early on the morning of June 6 from the effects of the gunshot wounds he had received.

The days that followed were filled with memorable scenes as Kennedy's body was carried to New York for a requiem mass and then taken by train to Washington, D.C., for burial at Arlington National Cemetery. Thousands of people lined the route of the train, and two women were killed when they spilled onto the track in the way of trains going in the other direction. Politicians adjourned the campaign for a few days, and the press explored the phenomenon of growing social violence in the United States. The death of Robert Kennedy, like that of Martin Luther King, Jr., came to symbolize the anguish of a year when shock followed shock in bewildering succession.

Robert Kennedy's death in the midst of the campaign left unanswered forever the question of whether he could have defeated Hubert Humphrey for the Democratic nomination. Friends of the senator later claimed he had a good chance, arguing that Humphrey's delegate strength, while impressive on paper, was soft. "Humphrey had a lot of delegates," said one McCarthy backer, "but not enough to win." According to this view, a determined Kennedy, campaigning with his frenetic energy, could have swayed wavering Humphrey support and united with McCarthy backers to win the nomination.

In the years after Kennedy's death a related argument arose: only he among the Democratic candidates in 1968 could have rebuilt the coalition of white ethnic voters and blacks that had won for John Kennedy in 1960. In this scenario, Robert Kennedy could have reached across barriers of class and race to unify disadvantaged whites and disaffected minorities and staved off the Republican dominance of the 1970s and 1980s. This romantic vision especially appealed to liberal Democrats in the years when their fortunes in electoral politics were bleak.

No one can say for sure what would have happened had Kennedy lived, but the evidence suggests that his unifying abilities would have been inadequate to the task that confronted the Democrats in 1968. Despite his enthusiastic crowds, Kennedy lacked popularity with the broad mass of voters. In much of the South, animosity toward him was intense. Had he won the Democratic nomination, it is hard, for example, to visualize him winning the state of Texas. Humphrey did so in the fall, in part because of George Wallace and also because Lyndon Johnson and John Connally pulled the warring Texas Democrats together for their party's candidate. It is inconceivable that such efforts would have been made on behalf of the presidential candidacy of Robert Kennedy. Kennedy's advocates use his success at winning a plurality of Democratic voters as proof that he would have been a strong national candidate in the fall election. More plausibly, he would not have run as well as Humphrey did in November 1968.

After Kennedy's death the lineup for the fall elections seemed assured. Nixon was well in front for the Republican nomination, Humphrey would win when the Democrats met in Chicago in late August, and the Wallace third-party candidacy would be in the field as an unknown and potentially powerful element. Beneath the surface, however, all was not as secure as it seemed. Humphrey had the problem of Lyndon Johnson to address if he was to be a successful candidate. Richard Nixon faced a possible challenge from the popular Ronald Reagan. Finally, George Wallace had to show that he was more than a wasted third-party vote. The summer of 1968 proved as volatile and complex as the violent spring.

4

Nixon's the One

THE MURDER of Robert Kennedy had no serious impact on the campaign of George Wallace or Richard Nixon. It left the Democratic situation in continuing turmoil. The party seemed unable to find a secure place from which to prepare for the fall contest against the Republicans.

For Eugene McCarthy, the personal effects of the assassination were the most devastating. His candidacy never recovered from the shock of what happened in Los Angeles. He said later that his goal "after the primaries" was to create "sufficient strength" to ensure that the Vietnam issue received a full airing at the Democratic National Convention. He hoped in the end to induce Hubert Humphrey to break with Lyndon Johnson over the war. McCarthy seems to have recognized in early June that he probably could not deny the vice president the nomination.

McCarthy's personal course during the summer of 1968 helped assure Humphrey's nomination, but it also limited the ability of anti-war Democrats to influence the convention. For McCarthy to have a powerful impact on the delegates, he needed to keep his own candidacy viable. Instead the Minnesota senator "withdrew" as a committed participant in the nomination process. Nothing formal was ever said, but, as one of his speech writers noted bitterly, "Gene McCarthy regressed to his balanced presentation of self, to the sacred ceremony of his personality."

During the weeks of June and July McCarthy distanced himself from his campaign and the exuberant supporters who still yearned to go all out for him. He made no positive overtures to the former supporters of Robert Kennedy. He refused to court governors and other Democratic leaders who might have come out for him against Humphrey. He ruled out efforts to woo wavering Humphrey delegates, either in behind-the-scenes negotiations or through public speeches against the vice president's candidacy. The senator also declined to go into the cities and appeal to black voters who had been so strong for Robert Kennedy. McCarthy complained that the presidential nominating process was endless and unrewarding. "It's as if someone gave you the football and you're running with it, but the field never ends."

A few positive moments indicated the residual power of McCarthy's cause. On June 18 his forces won the Democratic primary in New York and received sixty-two delegate votes. Victory in that state required extensive grassroots organizing because the New York party mandated a complicated selection process. It was a testament to the enthusiasm that liberal, antiwar Democrats still brought to McCarthy's candidacy. Elsewhere Humphrey's dominance of the party machinery produced triumphs for the vice president in the Connecticut, Montana, and Minnesota conventions. Similar results occurred in Kentucky, Texas, and Washington. McCarthy's supporters focused on the way the Democratic nominating system, using a "unit rule" that ceded all votes in a delegation to the majority, denied representation to a defeated minority.

Some of these complaints were self-serving. In those states where McCarthy's people won control, they had no qualms about giving their man all the available votes. In local conventions in Minnesota, for example, longtime Democratic leaders found themselves stripped of their power. Nonetheless the newcomers to politics who made up most of McCarthy's following were outraged at party rules that allowed Humphrey's campaign to use such tactics against their candidate.

Kennedy's death shook Hubert Humphrey as well, and he failed to make good use of the months of June, July, and August to strengthen his campaign organization and to find workable themes for the fall election. One of the vice president's abiding concerns was money for his campaign. After Kennedy died, the large contributors who had supported Humphrey with such generosity in April and May returned to their customary Republican allegiance. In late June the Humphrey campaign fired fifty campaign workers from its payroll to save money. A month later the fall advertising strategy fell behind schedule because the campaign had failed to make an initial payment to its New York advertising agency.

Once Humphrey became the clear front-runner, he also emerged as a lightning rod for demonstrations and heckling from the more virulent anti-war groups. The cry was "Dump the Hump," and signs linked the vice president with Johnson: "Why Change the Ventriloquist for the Dummy?" Other protesters told Humphrey, "Wash the blood off your hands." Humphrey's response to these attacks, while spirited at times, lacked the edge that Wallace imparted to his replies to heckling. As one of Humphrey's aides recalled, the vice president "became associated in the American mind with unruliness, loud demonstrations, that kind of thing."

A British reporter noted about the Humphrey campaign after a July 4 address in Philadelphia: "There is an unmistakable whiff of mediocrity about the Humphrey operation these days." Much of the difficulty lay in Humphrey's organization. The dual leadership of Fred Harris and Walter Mondale had not worked well. Too many Humphrey friends played a part in the campaign without defined responsibilities. The candidate sought to recruit Lawrence O'Brien to play a large role in the organization, but even when O'Brien joined the campaign there were still no clear lines of authority.

The central problem for Humphrey was his relationship to Lyndon Johnson and his position on the war in Vietnam. If the vice president presented himself as a duplicate of the president, he would inherit all the animosities toward Johnson within the Democratic party and the nation. Yet to split with the president risked a public repudiation and perhaps Johnson's own reentry into the race. Taking a position different from the administration on Vietnam also raised the prospect of attacks on Humphrey for undermining the war effort at a crucial point in the negotiations then under way in Paris.

At some basic level, Humphrey was afraid of Lyndon Johnson. The president had a streak of sadistic cruelty in his personality that he often vented against Humphrey. He told Joseph Califano, a White House aide, that Humphrey had "Minnesota running water disease. I've never known anyone from Minnesota that could keep their mouth shut." He had promised Humphrey in 1964 that the vice president would have an important role in the administration but then did all he could to turn Humphrey into a docile and quiet presence. "With Johnson," said a Humphrey worker, "it was either a bear hug or a kick in the ass." Humphrey had decided in 1965 that he was "going to be absolutely loyal to Lyndon Johnson come what may." Now his future depended on breaking those ties and establishing himself as his own man.

Humphrey held some advantages in a possible confrontation. Johnson could not fire him as vice president, and being the object of the president's wrath would arouse public sympathy. The act of defiance would underline Humphrey's personal courage. But none of these considerations swayed Humphrey. He could not summon the nerve to confront Johnson on the issue. "I'm in the position of walking on a tightrope," he said that summer.

Lyndon Johnson did not make Humphrey's political life any easier during these months. Having renounced the presidency and the power he loved, Johnson sought to achieve a Vietnam settlement on his own terms. He did not wish to see the Democratic party and its candidate undercut the White House, and he exercised presidential influence to keep Humphrey in line with the administration. One act of self-denial in 1968 was all that Lyndon Johnson could muster.

One way Johnson damaged his vice president was in the Supreme Court appointments he announced in late June. Chief Justice Earl Warren had informed the president that he intended to resign. To succeed the liberal chief justice, Johnson decided to elevate his old friend Abe Fortas, already an associate justice on the Court. Since promoting Fortas would leave a vacancy, Johnson decided to nominate another close friend, Homer Thornberry of the Fifth Circuit Court of Appeals. The president regarded Fortas as a man of superior intellect, and Johnson believed he could thus influence the direction of the Court well into the future. Since the Senate had already confirmed Fortas for the Supreme Court and Thornberry for a federal judgeship, Johnson reasoned that a majority of senators could hardly balk at this package deal. When Clark Clifford expressed doubts about getting the two men through the Senate, and suggested pairing Fortas with a Republican, Johnson responded, "Well, I don't intend to put some damned Republican on the Court."

Johnson had miscalculated. Both Fortas and Thornberry were politically vulnerable. Fortas had alienated the right wing of the Republican party by representing alleged Communists during the 1950s and by some of his decisions on the Court. An equally important weakness was the intimate working relationship he had maintained with Johnson even while Fortas was a sitting justice. He had advised the president on Vietnam policy, drafted speeches, and participated in other policy deliberations.

Neither Fortas nor Johnson had been sensitive to the proprieties of his judicial position. Charges of cronyism thus had a good deal of substance. In a different sense, the same allegation could be made about Homer Thornberry. He was a decent man whose abilities did not mark him out for a Supreme Court appointment; his rise had been based on his friendship with the president.

In the larger context of 1968, the Fortas nomination offered Republicans a chance to talk about the rulings of the Supreme Court, particularly in the area of criminal law. During the 1960s the Court had expanded the rights of the accused in such cases as *Miranda v. Arizona* (1966), in which the Court held that potential criminal defendants must be informed of their rights before being questioned by the police. Fortas was one of the majority votes in *Miranda*. Before his appointment to the Court, Fortas had defended Clarence Earl Gideon in another case that established the right of every defendant to legal representation.

Nixon did not criticize the Fortas appointment himself. He did not have to. Statements such as the one he made to the platform committee of the Republican National Convention sounded the theme in general terms. "At every level of law enforcement and criminal justice," he wrote, "there are needed men with an awareness of the crime crisis, men with a new attitude toward crime and criminals." Conservative Republicans knew that Nixon would support their attack on Fortas.

Johnson lined up Senate votes for his choices, including Republican leader Everett Dirksen of Illinois. Opposition to Fortas appeared, however, among other Republican senators, the most notable of whom was Robert P. Griffin of Michigan. He argued that a lame-duck president should not have the right to select two Supreme Court justices. Criticism also focused on Fortas's decisions and on the general issue of "cronyism." Richard Nixon told reporters, "It would have been wise for the President to have delayed the appointment . . . until the new President had been elected."

In the context of electoral politics, the Fortas nomination convinced Republicans that a wheeler-dealer president was attempting to put something over on their party before the voters could speak. The Senate hearings on Fortas's qualifications allowed Republicans such as Strom Thurmond to work over the issues of liberal "permissiveness" and crime in the streets to the detriment of Democrats. The last thing Hubert Humphrey needed was to have Lyndon Johnson give the Republicans another reason to be united in their quest for the White House.

Humphrey's clumsy efforts to distance himself from Johnson over Vietnam failed in the weeks before the Democratic National Convention. He indicated to reporters that he would soon make an important statement on the war. A group of advisers had been working on a draft pronouncement for a month, and on July 25 they hammered out a final version. In it Humphrey was to say that given positive action by the enemy, "I would favor an immediate halt to the bombing of North Vietnam."

Humphrey took the draft statement to Johnson that evening, and the president threw cold water on Humphrey's initiative. As Humphrey related it, Johnson told him "that I would be jeopardizing the lives of his sons-in-law (then assigned to duty in Vietnam), and endangering the chances of peace. If I announced this, he'd destroy me for the Presidency." A battered Humphrey returned to his aides with the lame excuse that Johnson had been entertaining guests and could not discuss the statement.

Two weeks later, on August 9, Humphrey and Johnson met again at the Johnson ranch in Texas. Richard Nixon had been nominated for president by the Republicans a day earlier. A new draft of a Vietnam statement had been prepared for Humphrey to show the president. It called for an end to the bombing of North Vietnam when the other side showed "reciprocity." Again

Johnson was scathing: "You can get a headline with this, Hubert, and it will please you and some of your friends. But if you just let me work for peace, you'll have a better chance for election than by any speech you're going to make. I think I can pull it off. I think that I possibly can get negotiations going, and possibly get the beginnings of peace." With this Hubert Humphrey had to be content as the national convention neared in late August.

While Humphrey struggled with his Vietnam demons, Richard Nixon had moved toward what seemed an inevitable nomination at the Republican National Convention in Miami Beach. At fifty-five years of age, Nixon knew that 1968 would be his last chance at the White House. If he lost another presidential race, there was no possibility the Republicans would turn to him again. Nixon had been a rising young Republican politician during the late 1940s and early 1950s, and that had enabled him to become Eisenhower's running mate in 1952. Early in his career, Nixon was a hard-hitting partisan who waged aggressive, often dirty campaigns against his Democratic opponents. Memories of his use of anti-communism tactics to defeat Helen Gahagan Douglas in the 1950 Senate race in California still riled older Democrats. During the 1950s Nixon had carried the banners of conservative Republicanism in congressional elections while President Eisenhower remained above the political battles. His narrow defeat at the hands of John Kennedy in 1960 and the loss of the California governorship in 1962 had given him a "loser" image that he struggled hard to overcome during the first half of 1968.

Richard Nixon has been the subject of political and personal analysis for more than six decades. In 1968 that process was intense. Had a "New Nixon," the press asked, replaced the "Old Nixon" of the 1950s? The candidate was aware of his problem. "They still call me 'Tricky Dick.' It's a brutal thing to fight . . .," he said in 1967. The only way he could counter the impression of being devious, Nixon added, was "by absolute candor."

In its handling of the press, the Nixon campaign sought the appearance of candor in the context of tight control. During the primaries, Nixon's men found that putting their candidate before favorable audiences that posed friendly questions worked well. The resulting footage made for commercials that presented the candidate in a positive and attractive light. As one aide put it, without irony, they sought to emphasize Nixon's spontaneity, which they could then "capture and capsule."

Because of his lead among Republicans, Nixon could focus on general election issues. The primaries enabled him to test and develop themes for the fall in a way that Hubert Humphrey never could. The relative absence of internal warfare among the Republicans was an important element in their favor in 1968. It also promised Nixon a united party during the fall campaign, an advantage denied to Humphrey.

After his many years devoted to politics and party, Nixon could count on a network of loyal supporters among Republicans across the country. He was, wrote the novelist Norman Mailer, "the representative" of the "conservative orderly heart" of Midwestern and Far Western Republicanism. Nonetheless his candidacy aroused more respect than enthusiasm within the GOP in 1968. He was "the one" for the Republicans that year in order to avoid the hated Rockefeller. Many in the South preferred to give their hearts to the more exciting and charismatic Ronald Reagan.

To pursue the presidency, Nixon had assembled a campaign organization designed to avoid the mistakes he had made eight years earlier. "We started Nixon off in 1960 sick and under medication and then we ran his tail off," wrote H. R. Haldeman, one of his senior advisers. It was an error that Nixon and the men around him were determined not to repeat. Their operation also had the luxury of ample resources, with some $10 million available during the preconvention phase of the campaign. Even after a lifetime in politics, the reclusive Nixon did not relish the process of seeking the presidency. When an aide asked if he enjoyed the campaign, the candidate responded, "Never do. Campaigns are something to get over with."

The delegate selection process seemed to favor him in a large way. Nelson Rockefeller's expensive attempt to show Nixon's weaknesses in the polls had produced no significant results. Meanwhile, delegates moved toward Nixon. He won the Illinois primary and did well in the New Mexico, Washington, and Montana state conventions. Capping the favorable trend, former president Dwight D. Eisenhower endorsed him on July 18. From his sickbed in Washington, Eisenhower told the press of his "admiration of [Nixon's] personal qualities."

With the nomination in hand, Nixon had time to work on his acceptance speech and think about his running mate. Nixon wanted his vice-presidential candidate to be more effective than Henry Cabot Lodge had been in 1960. On several occasions Lodge had embarrassed Nixon and hurt the campaign against Kennedy. One name that came up often in Nixon's inner circle was that of Spiro T. Agnew, the governor of Maryland. The idea was tucked away for future consideration.

As summer progressed, Nixon pursued his campaign on several different levels. In addition to winning delegates, he looked ahead to the general election. What Nixon most feared was that Lyndon Johnson might achieve the appearance of peace in Vietnam on the eve of the election. Accordingly, Nixon moved to identify himself with the goals of the president's policy on Vietnam, "even though I would be critical of some of the tactics that had been used." Nixon received an intelligence briefing at the White House on July 26, a courtesy that Johnson provided to all the presidential hopefuls. Nixon told the president he would not "undercut our negotiating position just in case the Communists came around and agreed to the conditions Johnson would insist upon in return for a bombing halt." A day earlier Johnson had quashed Humphrey's effort to separate himself from the administration in Vietnam. Now here was Nixon seeming to support the White House. Two days before Nixon's visit, Johnson told Clark Clifford and Dean Rusk, "The GOP may be of more help to us than the Democrats in the next few months." What Nixon said strengthened Johnson's view that he was closer to the president's position than was Humphrey.

Johnson did not know that Nixon and his campaign had already made a contact with Vietnam that would prove crucial during the waning days of the election. Anna Chennault was the widow of General Claire Chennault, who had led the famous Flying Tigers squadron in China during World War II. Of Chinese ancestry, Mrs. Chennault had become identified with the Republican party during the 1960s, and she counted many friends among South Vietnamese political leaders in Saigon and Washington. In late June she wrote to candidate Nixon saying that the ambassador to the United States from South Vietnam, Bui Diem, was "my close friend." She urged Nixon to meet with him. Nixon told aides that "if it can be [secret]" he would like to see Diem. If secrecy could not be maintained, an aide would handle the meeting. According to Mrs. Chennault's memoir, Nixon had already met the ambassador some months earlier. In any event, the channel was well established by midsummer 1968, to be used in case Nixon need to convey a private message to the South Vietnamese government. As Nixon told Bui Diem, "If you have any message for me, please give it to Anna and she will relay it to me and I will do the same in the future."

For the moment, however, Nixon's thoughts were on the Republican convention to be held August 5 to 9. While his managers assured him, as John Mitchell said, that "we've got everything under control," the candidate knew that Nelson Rockefeller and

Ronald Reagan were maneuvering to show delegates that Nixon could be stopped, that a first-ballot victory was not a foregone conclusion. As the convention neared, Nixon knew that Rockefeller's challenge would fail. Despite the money the New York governor had thrown into his polling campaign, in Nixon's words, "his efforts seemed to have minimal effect." The potential of a Reagan candidacy was more worrisome. Throughout the primary campaign, Reagan had always been perceived as the main alternative to a Nixon nomination.

Ronald Reagan had burst upon the national political scene in 1966 when he defeated the incumbent Democratic governor of California, Edmund G. "Pat" Brown, by almost a million votes. His ability to thrill the hearts of conservative Republicans had been evident two years earlier when his televised speech in favor of Barry Goldwater had been the hit of the faltering Republican presidential campaign. A former Democrat who had become famous as an actor in movies and television, Reagan was a gifted speaker with an ability to state the conservative creed in crisp and forceful phrases. "There are simple answers," he told Californians in 1966, "just not easy ones." He promised a smaller state government, lower taxes, and a crackdown on those who abused welfare and other government programs. His smashing victory over Brown gave Reagan instant visibility as a potential Republican presidential candidate.

Reagan came to the California governorship with no experience in governance, and in his first two years he suffered some rocky moments. In 1967 he was forced to seek a significant tax increase from the legislature to pay for the increasing costs of state services that resisted his economy measures that had seemed so attractive in the campaign. In that same year a scandal uncovered gays on the governor's staff. Nonetheless Reagan demonstrated striking abilities as a fund-raiser among Republicans; he could bring in several hundred thousand dollars during a swing through several states. His rhetoric stirred the blood of the party faithful. "We can't really blame the President alone for the mess we're in," he jibed. "A mess like that takes teamwork."

Reagan had no desire to take on Nixon directly in 1968. He had said during his campaign that he would not use the governorship as a stepping-stone to the presidency. He controlled the large California delegation to the national convention, and as a "favorite son" his name would be placed in nomination whether he campaigned or not. Yet if he were perceived as a declared candidate, he would be measured against Nixon in the polls, where he was bound to look weak relative to the front-runner. His best approach was to accept the many speaking invitations that came his way, raise money for the party, and allow his friends to engage in a quiet courtship of potential delegates on his behalf. If Nixon ran into trouble, or if a deadlocked convention loomed, Reagan's candidacy would prosper.

The Reagan campaign moved with caution during the early months of 1968. His name appeared on the ballot in those states where officials moved to place it, and he declined to insist that his name be removed. Reagan gained 11 percent of the vote in Wisconsin's primary in April, rose to 22 percent in the Nebraska primary, and prepared to do even better in the Oregon balloting in late May. Reagan supporters spent some $200,000 on television advertising in Oregon, including a document, "Ronald Reagan, Citizen Governor." But the Reagan drive stalled when the governor received only 23 percent of the vote to Nixon's 73 percent. Despite this setback, Reagan continued to be a threat to Nixon's chances. "There was always a possibility," Nixon wrote later, "that Southern delegates could be lured at the last minute by his ideological siren song."

During the week before the start of the Republican convention, the platform committee debated how the party should approach the issues before the voters. Under the leadership of

Senator Dirksen, the GOP offered stern criticism of Lyndon Johnson's domestic policies while adopting a cautious line on the Vietnam War. "Lawlessness is crumbling the foundations of American society," the Republican platform asserted, and it pledged "vigorous and evenhanded administration of justice and enforcement of the law." As for Vietnam, the party advocated "a program for peace" that would be "neither peace at any price nor a camouflaged surrender of legitimate United States or allied interests." Instead the Republicans promised "a fair and equitable settlement to all, based on the principle of self-determination, our national interests and the cause of long-range world peace." They also said their course would "enable and induce South Vietnam to assume increasing responsibility." The goal was "a progressive de-Americanization of the war, both military and civilian." Rather than calling for further U.S. prosecution of the war, the Republican platform advocated what Richard Nixon would later describe as "Vietnamization" of the conflict.

As the convention prepared to open on August 5, Ronald Reagan made his unofficial candidacy official. In a staged event with the California delegation, his supporters adopted a resolution that asked the governor to become "a leading and bona fide candidate for President." Reagan walked in and commented, "Gosh, I was surprised. It all came out of the clear blue sky." Now the issue turned on whether Reagan could break into Nixon's support among Southern Republicans. Reagan's campaign manager, F. Clifton White, told reporters, "All we need is just one break—one state switching to Reagan—and we've got him."

The strategy for Nixon's two main opponents was to prevent his victory on the first ballot. If they could do that, the strength of the front-runner would wane and compromise candidates could emerge. Nelson Rockefeller believed he would then win in the end. A more likely scenario, given the anti-Rockefeller passion

that ran through the convention, would have been a Reagan triumph. For the moment, however, there was an uneasy and un-
spoken alliance against Nixon between the moderate Rockefeller
and the conservative Reagan.

The issue on which the well-organized Nixon operation could
falter was the vice presidency. If he decided to select a Northern
liberal, such as John Lindsay of New York or Mark Hatfield of
Oregon, unhappy Southerners might defect and switch their votes
to Reagan. Newspaper stories circulated that Lindsay and Hatfield were under active consideration. Such trial balloons from the
Nixon camp triggered fear among the conservative Southern delegates, and by Monday evening, August 5, the Nixon camp was
hearing reports of possible gains for Reagan in the South. When
the leader of the North Carolina delegation told Nixon operatives,
"I'm for Ronnie," concern rose among members of the Nixon
high command. Southern supporters warned of a need "to see
Nixon tonight" because "things are taking a turn for the worse."

That evening Nixon met with Strom Thurmond and Harry
Dent of South Carolina and repeated his pledges that the vice-
presidential nominee would be someone acceptable to the South.
He also reaffirmed that he opposed "civil wrongs" and would appoint an attorney general "who'll enforce the law!" On the emotional issue of how to desegregate schools in the South, Nixon
made clear his firm opposition to busing. His visitors told Nixon
to repeat those same positions to Southern delegates when he
met with them the next morning.

How Nixon handled the racial question would be central to
the success of his campaign. To appeal to the South, especially
the border states, he had to be more conciliatory to whites than
Hubert Humphrey would be. At the same time he could not
outbid George Wallace for racist voters North and South or he
would face an uproar among Northern Republicans and mod-

erate Democrats. What Nixon did was to reaffirm his support for the principle of integration in general but remain cautious about the use of federal power to push racial change. His emphasis rested on voluntary compliance by the South with an even-handed racial policy.

To avoid being trapped at either extreme of the racial question, Nixon had spoken in favor of the open-housing legislation proposed by the White House after the death of Martin Luther King. Nixon was not an admirer of open housing, but he thought, as he later informed Southern delegates, that it was best "to get the civil rights and open-housing issues out of our sight so we didn't have a split party over the platform when we came down here to Miami Beach."

On the issues of school desegregation and busing, circumstances played into Nixon's hands during the spring of 1968. The Supreme Court ruled in May that the "freedom of choice" approach to school integration had failed to end dual school systems in the South. It was not enough for parents to have the right to choose where their children would go to school. To end segregation it would be necessary, the decision seemed to say, to transport children to other schools in the district in order to achieve proper racial balance.

In light of the Court's decision, Southern Republicans were exercised about the prospect of the federal government setting "guidelines" for the pursuit of integration. Nixon worked out a strategy designed to say just what his white backers in the South wanted to hear without descending to the levels where George Wallace operated so well. At meetings with Southern delegates, Nixon ran through his positions with the skill he had so often displayed in such group meetings. One of the delegates carried a small tape recorder, and the candidate's remarks were preserved and published the next day in the *Miami Herald*.

Nixon said first that he would not select anyone as his running mate who "is going to divide the party." On busing, he assured delegates that he opposed moving "the child—a child that
is two or three grades behind another child into a strange community." He attacked federal judges who overruled the decisions
of local school districts or school boards: "I think it is the job of
the courts to interpret the law, and not make the law." On Vietnam he promised "a massive training program so that the South
Vietnamese can be trained to take over the fighting—that they
can be phased in as we phase out."

The sessions with the Southern delegates on Monday went
even better than the Nixon camp might have anticipated. By the
time Nixon finished, Reagan's hoped-for gains in Southern support had been largely canceled. It was clear that Thurmond and
other Nixon supporters would be able to deliver the Southern
Republicans for him on the first ballot. On Tuesday Reagan tried
to sway Thurmond without success. As the delegates prepared
to vote on Wednesday, August 7, it looked as though Nixon had
withstood the Reagan challenge.

But pitfalls remained. When the Florida delegation began
to waver, Strom Thurmond had to make a personal visit to ask
them to hold off on their sentiment for Ronald Reagan. Similar
signs of Reagan sentiment appeared within the Alabama delegation. To compensate for any losses in the South, the Nixon
campaign made inroads into the New Jersey delegation to
draw off potential Rockefeller support. Even as the nominating
speeches began, another round of Reagan sentiment surfaced
when the *Miami Herald* reported that Nixon would select Mark
Hatfield as his running mate. Nixon leaders in the South confronted the reporter who had written the story and challenged
him to bet several hundred dollars on its accuracy. When the
reporter refused, the news spread among Nixon supporters in
Dixie.

Republicans spent ten hours nominating their candidate. Spiro T. Agnew of Maryland endorsed Nixon as a man "firm in upholding the law and determined in the pursuit of justice." Nixon "knows what is needed to be President and he knows what a President needs to be." Reagan and Rockefeller were also placed in nomination, along with a bevy of favorite-son candidates. When the balloting took place, the states fell into line as the Nixon people had forecast. The final totals gave Nixon 692 votes to 277 for Rockefeller and 182 for Reagan. Nixon had won the nomination with 25 votes to spare.

Nixon watched the voting on television in his hotel suite, tabulating the totals on one of the yellow pads he used for drafting memos and speeches. "We had come halfway up the mountain," he said later. Congratulatory telephone calls soon flowed in, including one from Nelson Rockefeller who told him that Reagan "didn't come through as well as we expected."

The first task for the Republican nominee was the selection of his vice-presidential candidate. Although Nixon had decided several weeks before the convention that Agnew was the likely choice, "like most important decisions, this one would not be final until it was announced." Nixon very much wanted to avoid duplicating the mistake he had made in 1960 when he selected Henry Cabot Lodge, Jr. In 1968 the vice-presidential choice should be someone who would help the ticket, attract votes in the South and border states, and follow the lead of the Nixon campaign.

In 1968 Spiro Agnew seemed to have the needed qualities. He was fifty years old, the son of Greek immigrant parents, and a veteran of World War II who had practiced law in Maryland during the 1950s. In 1960 he decided to enter Republican politics and ran unsuccessfully for a state judgeship. He was elected a county executive in Baltimore in 1962 and ran for governor four years later. In the election campaign Agnew's opponent, George

P. Mahoney, was a Democrat who opposed the integration of housing in the state. His slogan was "Your Home Is Your Castle." Mahoney's segregationist posture split the Democrats and opened the way for the election of the more moderate Agnew.

In 1968 Agnew seemed a likely supporter of Nelson Rockefeller. He was one of the few Republican governors who were prepared to make a public endorsement of the New Yorker during the spring. Then Rockefeller suddenly decided on March 21 not to make the race. Before he made the announcement, he did not call Agnew and prepare him for what was about to happen. As a result, Agnew was embarrassed. He had invited reporters to his office to see the anticipated Rockefeller entrance into the race. Instead he was humiliated. "It made him look like a horse's ass," said one Republican. Agnew began to move toward Nixon. He also changed his mind about some of the racial issues that had brought him to the governor's office.

After the death of Martin Luther King, Maryland had its share of rioting in the wake of the assassination. Agnew mobilized the National Guard and requested federal troops to maintain order in the state. At a meeting with black leaders in his office, Agnew scolded them for their behavior and accused them of being parties to the rioting. Most of the blacks in attendance walked out of the session. Agnew followed up with statements that showed his new feelings. "Policemen ought to shoot looters who fail to halt when ordered," he said. He also charged that urban rioting grew out of "the misguided compassion of public opinion." A governor who had won election against a segregationist was now saying that crime and permissiveness should receive harsh punishment. It was a combination that "fit perfectly with the strategy we had devised for the November election," Nixon recalled.

Nixon had weighed Agnew's political strengths and weaknesses with a masterful sense of political reality. Despite the importance of the vice presidency as a national office, however, Nixon ordered no probe of Agnew's private affairs or his finances. Nor did Nixon ask him whether he had any potential scandals that might affect his fitness to be vice president. It was a significant oversight. During Nixon's presidency, federal investigators discovered evidence that Agnew was involved in conspiracies to commit bribery, extortion, and tax fraud. During his service in Maryland government, Agnew had received regular payments and kickbacks from contractors in his state. These funds flowed in while Agnew was a vice-presidential candidate and even during his service in the Nixon administration. In 1973 they would lead to Agnew's resignation as vice president.

In August 1968, however, the issue was how Agnew would help the Nixon candidacy. Nixon offered the vice-presidential slot first to his old friend from California, Robert Finch, but Finch declined. Nixon then asked Congressman Rogers Morton from Maryland. Morton also said no, arguing that "Ted [Agnew] would be the stronger candidate." Nixon then settled on Agnew, announcing it on August 8 to a press corps that reacted with "absolute shock and surprise." A brief flurry of opposition to Agnew appeared in the convention, but it soon disappeared. His opponents mustered only 178 delegates against the nomination.

Agnew's selection proved to be a source of trouble for Nixon during the campaign. Agnew had a tendency to speak without thinking, and his off-the-cuff remarks produced several gaffes that Democrats exploited. It is not clear that Agnew added much strength to the ticket, though he may have been helpful in the border states.

For Nixon, the climax of the national convention was to be his speech accepting the nomination. No campaign speech, he said, would have "a larger or more attentive audience." Events outside the convention hall reinforced the arguments Nixon would make. The night before, while Nixon's nomination was being won, blacks in nearby Miami's Liberty City ghetto had rioted. Three black residents died, and troops were called into the area to put down looting and sniping. The episode symbolized the tensions within the nation in 1968. In the opulent confines of Miami Beach, well protected from any disturbances, the delegates went about choosing the next president; ten miles away, the social problems of the nation burst open once again.

Nixon's acceptance speech was a mixture of his familiar campaign address and personal comments about his own life. The product of many speech writers, it reflected Nixon's perceptions about what the voters wanted to hear from a Republican candidate. He spoke for "the great majority of Americans, the forgotten Americans, the non-shouters, the non-demonstrators." He then made the case for "new leadership." The nation was "tied down for four years in a war in Vietnam with no end in sight." The United States could not "manage its own economy" and was "plagued by unprecedented racial violence." He jabbed at Johnson and the Great Society without mentioning the president's name. "I say it's time to quit pouring billions of dollars into programs that have failed." He promised to appoint a new attorney general who would be tough on crime.

In closing he invoked the plight of children who failed to benefit from the American dream. When those children awoke each morning, he said, they encountered "a living nightmare of poverty, neglect, and despair." Having sketched that difficult social problem, he then turned to the story of another child who "hears a train go by. At night he dreams of faraway places where he'd like to go. It seems like an impossible dream." But with the help of family and friends, Richard Nixon prevailed in "his chosen profession of politics," and "tonight he stands before you, nominated for President of the United States of America."

The Republican convention had done everything Nixon wanted it to accomplish. The party was united behind his candidacy, and there had been no major divisive battle to weaken the national campaign. Nixon received what poll takers called "a bounce" from the convention. He held a strong lead of 45 percent to 29 percent over Hubert Humphrey in the Gallup poll. George Wallace trailed with 18 percent of the vote. The choice of Agnew had aroused some controversy, but Nixon expected that his running mate would help offset Wallace in the states of the upper South.

By 1968 the Republican party was on the verge of dominating the competition for electoral votes. In much of the West the Republicans had little to fear from the Democrats. Nixon could reasonably expect to start out with as many as 65 to 70 electoral votes in the Far West and Great Plains states. He was also all but assured of the votes of such Midwestern states as Iowa, Indiana, and Ohio. He hoped to run well in the industrial states of New York, Illinois, Pennsylvania, and Michigan, and he was intent on carrying California and Texas. The key to Nixon's chances lay in the South. If he could blunt the challenge of George Wallace, he would gain the 268 electoral votes he needed for election.

Turning back the Wallace candidacy would not be easy. Southern republicans warned Nixon that Wallace was doing well with voters who would otherwise support the GOP. Nixon knew he could not outbid Wallace on the race issue; his task was to persuade voters that casting their ballot for Wallace was futile. "Our message to would-be Wallace voters," Nixon remembered, "was 'Don't Waste Your Vote.'"

The Nixon campaign was well financed. The Republican party contributed something over $7 million, and the Nixon-Agnew campaign itself raised another $23 million. Nixon's finance director, Maurice Stans, later observed that "ours was the most expensive campaign ever." During the 1960s the base of small contributors developed by Ray Bliss gave Republicans a decided edge over the Democrats. In 1968 big contributors also poured in money to see that Republicans regained the White House. Clement Stone of Chicago, a friend of Nixon's, gave more than $200,000 while hotel magnate J. Willard Marriott added $103,000. Republicans had all the money they needed to wage a modern campaign in contrast to the underfunded Democrats. Nixon told his staff, "Be sure we outspend them on television, especially in the last three weeks. Remember '60—I never want to be outspent again."

Nixon and his men had ample reason to be confident as they surveyed the campaign after their party's convention. They had a well-tested organization, an effective candidate, and a disorganized opposition. Their advantages grew during the remainder of August as the Democrats moved toward a disastrous national convention. Yet there was an underlying weakness at the heart of the Nixon campaign that would prove significant as the election neared. As William Safire, a Nixon speech writer, observed, "Nixon was playing not to lose." His candidacy rested on the premise that the voters wanted a change from the Democrats and would inevitably turn to Nixon. Thus there was the ambiguous campaign slogan "Nixon's the One." The emptiness of the appeal was evident in the song that went everywhere with the candidate: "Nixon's the One/ Nixon's the One/ Nixon's the One for Me."

As long as the Nixon campaign was comfortably ahead in the polls and confident of success, the lack of a clear, positive message was irrelevant. But if Democrats found unity and purpose and began to close the gap on Republicans, the absence of a central theme might prove to be more of a problem than the Nixon men had anticipated. Such a problem seemed far away during the confident days of August 1968. "It is essential that we maintain the initiative," Nixon instructed his associates on September 5. "We must play the confident line from now until November, regardless of what developments occur."

As Republicans readied themselves for the fall campaign, Democrats prepared for their convention. Originally scheduled as a celebration of Lyndon Johnson's sixtieth birthday on August 27, the gathering was to be held in Chicago, where the city's colorful and domineering mayor, Richard J. Daley, could provide a friendly setting for what the president had assumed would be a consensus renomination. Such planning had preceded the striking events of 1968—Johnson's withdrawal, the murder of Robert Kennedy, the presumed nomination of Humphrey. Now the Democrats were meeting as a divided party with the prospect of bitter floor disputes and even more violent protests outside the convention hall. Yet even the most pessimistic Democrats could not have anticipated the trauma that awaited their party in Chicago.

5

Democratic Disaster at Chicago

BY MID-AUGUST Hubert Humphrey was on the verge of winning the Democratic presidential nomination. The vice president was well ahead of Eugene McCarthy in the polls and in the race for convention delegates. Journalists estimated that Humphrey had about 1,250 committed delegates and was within 70 votes of the 1,312 delegates he needed. McCarthy had at most 800 delegates and little chance of winning on his own. The death of Robert Kennedy had left the anti-war wing of the Democrats divided and frustrated.

Despite these favorable signs, Humphrey's position was vulnerable and uncertain. Following the Republican convention he trailed Richard Nixon by sixteen percentage points in the polls. His own campaign was disorganized and underfunded, and he had not been able to heal the splits in his party. Audiences at Humphrey's speeches were often hostile and jeering. Most important, the vice president still had not resolved his relationship to Lyndon Johnson and the president's war policies. Humphrey had almost no influence on the negotiations the White House was conducting with North Vietnam and the Soviet Union. He believed that if he broke with Johnson, the president could destroy his candidacy with ease.

At the same time Johnson had his own doubts about Humphrey's loyalty to his administration and his policies. In July the president had told his advisers that Nixon "may prove to be more responsible than the Democrats." When he saw a newspaper photograph of Humphrey and Eugene McCarthy each with a crying baby in his arms, Johnson remarked, "That's the way I feel when I look at the two candidates, like crying." Johnson's meeting with Nixon and Spiro Agnew on August 10 was friendly. The Republican candidate said he would not criticize him on the war if the president did not "soften" his position. Humphrey thus knew the dangers of challenging Johnson directly. Yet the closer he remained to the president, the worse his electoral position became.

Humphrey's other problem was the national convention in Chicago on August 26. The site and date for the convention had been set months earlier when Lyndon Johnson was still a likely candidate for reelection. Mayor Richard Daley had lobbied hard with the president during the fall of 1967 to have his city selected. The president could carry Illinois if the party met in Chicago, Daley contended. Although the television networks wanted to ease their expenses by having both parties meet in Miami, and though security would be easier in the Florida city, Johnson went with Daley and decided to hold the convention in Chicago in late August. Thus the delegates could celebrate Lyndon Johnson's sixtieth birthday on August 27.

In hindsight the choice of Chicago was a political disaster. The timing produced severe difficulties for Humphrey and the Democrats. The Republicans, meeting several weeks earlier, had plenty of time to launch their campaign in early September. Humphrey had only a weekend to ready himself for the traditional start of the campaign on Labor Day. Since the vice president and his staff had done virtually no planning for the general election before the convention, Democrats went into the decisive phase of the 1968 contest with no clear sense of their strategy to win the White House. An earlier convention would have given them time to raise money and to settle their plans.

In the weeks before the convention Democratic discontent intensified. Senator George S. McGovern of South Dakota entered the presidential race on August 10. Because of his closeness to the Kennedys, his candidacy seemed designed to hold the former supporters of Robert Kennedy together until the convention. There was now the hope among these delegates that Senator Edward M. Kennedy, the youngest Kennedy brother, might accept a draft. McGovern's announcement underlined the perception that neither Humphrey nor McCarthy had a strong appeal to the Kennedy faction of the party.

By August many liberal Democrats believed that the election could not be won unless their party moved away from the administration's position on Vietnam. Yet the president gave them little reason to expect a change in his views. He had conferred with President Nguyen Van Thieu of South Vietnam in mid-July in Hawaii. At a press conference Johnson characterized the "big rumors" that the meeting was "to discuss stopping the bombing or to pull out" as "just pure, absolute tommyrot and fiction." In other public statements he repeated his unwillingness to "order the cessation of unilateral acts of bombing of the infiltration routes" that the North Vietnamese used. On August 19, a week before the national convention, he told the Veterans of Foreign Wars in Detroit, "We are not going to stop the bombing just to give them [North Vietnam] a chance to step up their bloodbath."

Johnson's adamant stance did not deter prominent Democrats from searching for some way to have the party distance the nominee from the unpopular war. The McCarthy camp took the most radical position on the issue. Their proposed platform plank on Vietnam, announced on August 17, came out for an "unconditional end to all the bombing of South Vietnam," a negotiated withdrawal of all United States and North Vietnamese troops from South Vietnam, a coalition government in South Vietnam, and reduced military action on the battlefield. Johnson's Detroit speech indicated that the administration would never accept what McCarthy and his allies were proposing. The White House had firm control of the platform committee through its chair, Congressman Hale Boggs of Louisiana.

An effort continued, however, to find language that the anti-war faction could support, that Humphrey could run on, and that the White House would accept. Discussions opened on August 1 at a Washington hotel. A consensus emerged among the Kennedy men, McCarthy supporters, and McGovern delegates present that they had to be flexible and creative in working out platform language. By the time the platform committee convened on August 19, the advocates of a peace plan had worked out wording that Humphrey might find useful. The proposal included a call for an end to the bombing and a negotiated withdrawal from the war.

Outside events soon weakened the peace initiative. On August 20 Soviet troops invaded Czechoslovakia to extinguish its reformist government that had emerged during the "Prague spring." This aggressive move undercut Johnson's plans for an East-West summit. The president had hoped to announce agreements with Moscow as a way of emphasizing the peace issue in the campaign and ending his administration on an upbeat note. Worse still for the peace forces, the Soviet invasion strengthened the hand of those who contended that any negotiations with Communist governments were inherently dangerous. Senator McCarthy added to the political damage when he described the invasion as "not a major crisis." His assessment was accurate in a diplomatic sense—the United States could do nothing but protest the Soviet action; but the senator's words suggested that anti-war Democrats lacked a full appreciation of the dangers that confronted the United States in the summer of 1968.

In any event, Lyndon Johnson would not tolerate a platform critical of his Vietnam policy. He had his own plans for bringing about negotiations and an end to the bombing of North Vietnam, and he wanted no interference from liberal Democrats. Through his operatives on the scene in Chicago, including Postmaster General Marvin Watson, he made sure that the administration position was endorsed. On August 26, the day the convention opened, the president insisted that the language of the platform specify that any bombing halt would occur only "*when* this action would not endanger the lives of our troops in the field; this action should take into account the response from Hanoi." Critics of the president believed that this formulation offered the North Vietnamese slight incentive to accept.

In a conversation with Johnson that same day, Humphrey argued that the plank worked out between his aides and the liberals was "acceptable and not offensive." Johnson's response was simple and definitive: "This plank undercuts our whole policy and by God, the Democratic party ought not to be doing that to me, and you ought not to be doing it; you've been a part of this policy." Given how little influence Humphrey had exercised on Vietnam policy as vice president, this last assertion must have been ironic for him.

Humphrey briefly considered whether to make a determined stand on the platform issue. He retreated when Hale Boggs threatened to resign as chair of the platform committee if confronted with a plank that the president deemed unacceptable. In hindsight Humphrey wrote, "I should not have yielded." Worked on by Richard Nixon's shrewd courting of him on Vietnam, and defensive about his own place in history, the president showed little party loyalty by August 1968. He even toyed for a moment with the idea of being renominated if Humphrey faltered further. Wisely, Lyndon Johnson decided he could not go to the convention. His presence would have made an ugly situation even more explosive.

As it unfolded, the Democratic convention visited disaster after disaster on the party. Efforts to find an alternative to Humphrey led to a clumsy attempt to draft Senator Edward M. Kennedy of Massachusetts as the natural heir of the legacy of his two dead brothers. Grief-stricken by the year's events and aware of his own lack of qualifications for the presidency, the thirty-six-year-old Kennedy "simply could not summon the will" to accede to the sentiment for a draft that welled up in the weeks before the convention. In the end it came down to whether Eugene McCarthy would withdraw in favor of Kennedy. McCarthy said he would do it if his name were first placed in nomination. "While I am doing this for Teddy," he said to Kennedy's brother-in-law Stephen Smith, "I never could have done it for Bobby." The remark probably convinced Smith and Kennedy that they could not trust McCarthy to go through with such an understanding. On Wednesday, August 28, the third day of the convention, Kennedy telephoned Humphrey to say he would not be a candidate.

Edward Kennedy would never again be as close to the Democratic nomination as he was in August 1968, but it is doubtful that the draft would have been as easy as its adherents thought. Southern Democrats would not have accepted Kennedy under any circumstances, and Humphrey probably would have held on to enough votes to deny the Massachusetts senator the nomination. When the Kennedy boom ended, the chances of finding a liberal alternative to Humphrey also vanished.

The Democratic convention produced a series of political embarrassments for the party that weakened it over the next generation. As a result of the way in which Humphrey's delegates had been chosen in caucuses and state conventions, liberals believed that the party rules had become only a means of frustrating the will of Democrats nationally. They came to Chicago resolved to change the rules of the game, even if they did not succeed in 1968. A group of McCarthy supporters had established a commission to look into the methods of selecting delegates. In many areas there were apparent abuses. Delegates could be chosen up to two years before the convention, and in several states the exact nature of the nominating process was vague.

Particular attention focused on the so-called "unit rule" which allowed majorities in Southern states to control an entire delegation and shut out the party minority altogether. Blacks and liberals saw the unit rule as the last resort of such Southern conservatives as John Connally. The Humphrey camp first told Connally that the unit rule would remain in effect at the 1968 convention and be changed in the future. Then Connally learned that Humphrey, feeling pressure from Northern liberals, had endorsed the abolition of the rule "at this convention." An irate Connally began talking about a possible draft-Johnson movement. To avoid a divisive floor fight, the convention rules committee enacted a "freedom of conscience" provision which allowed delegates covered by the unit rule to vote as they thought best.

Other rules committee actions had even more far-reaching effects on the Democrats. Meeting on Tuesday, August 27, the committee set up a subcommittee to investigate how delegates were selected and to improve the process. A second subcommittee was empowered to look into enhancing the participation of all Democrats, whatever their religion, race, gender, or national origin. The convention approved these initiatives later that same day. During the four years after 1968, the work of these committees would transform the ways in which Democrats chose their presidential nominee. The goal was to make the party more open and more representative; the unintended consequence was to render Democrats less able to choose candidates who could win the White House.

The Democratic convention of 1968 is as famous for what oc-curred in the streets of Chicago during late August as for the events inside the hall that ended in the nomination of Hubert Humphrey. As police and anti-war protesters confronted each other, passions over the war in Vietnam reshaped national poli-tics with explosive impact. Television cameras carried the anger of the demonstrators and the response of the Chicago police into living rooms across the country. In a year of social unrest, the violence in Chicago symbolized the tensions that threatened to shatter the existing order.

As soon as the Democrats announced in late 1967 that their national convention would be held in Chicago, anti-war groups debated whether to stage protest demonstrations in the streets. A lack of money and people meant that only one of the major party conventions could be targeted, and the Democrats seemed the more compelling choice. Johnson was likely to be renominated; in the eyes of those who denounced the war, he was the chief vil-lain. As one of the more flamboyant protest leaders put it, "Chi-cago is LBJ's stage and we are going to steal it."

By early 1968 the peace movement against the Vietnam War had undergone important changes since its emergence on the na-tional scene in mid-1965. Two years of rallies, marches, and stu-dent protests had produced no discernible shift in the war policies of the Johnson administration. Behind the scenes, as the events of March 1968 showed, there was a good deal of anxiety within the White House about the course of the war. But the protesters saw only that the war they hated went on in Southeast Asia.

A climax to the mass-protest phase of the anti-war cam-paign came in October 1967 with the March on the Pentagon, organized by the National Mobilization to End the War. About 100,000 people came to Washington. A morning of speeches and entertainment at the Lincoln Memorial led to an afternoon walk to the Pentagon where a confrontation occurred with police and soldiers. Almost 650 marchers were arrested and a number of protesters were beaten. Angry that their tactics had produced no change in the war policy, leaders of the peace movement told one another that "one of our continuing aims must be to disrupt and block the war machine. . . . We might discuss the implications of trying to disrupt the nominating conventions of the Republican and Democratic parties."

The groups who planned to assemble in Chicago were diverse and often at cross-purposes with one another. The Youth International Party or "Yippies" attracted much media attention. The two leading figures of this small fringe organization were Jerry Rubin and Abbie Hoffman. They had been participants in the civil rights and anti-war efforts but had gradually become convinced that the movement needed new techniques and tactics to gain public attention and approval. Their goal, they said, was the "Politics of Ecstasy."

Abbie Hoffman was thirty-two in 1968, "a small wiry figure with a grotesque balloon of hair." After a degree from Brandeis University in 1959, he attended graduate school briefly and then worked for several years in a state mental hospital in Massachusetts. He spent time in civil rights and anti-war activities but was drawn to the world of drugs, rock, and what the 1960s called the "counterculture." He lost faith in conventional political organizing and turned instead to street theater, public relations stunts, and media manipulation. His goals were "Revolution for the hell of it!" and "Theater in the streets!"

At thirty, Jerry Rubin had shown himself to be an adept creator of the kinds of symbolic protests that Hoffman envisioned. A few inches shorter than his friend, Rubin had graduated from the University of Cincinnati, gone to graduate school at Berkeley for a few weeks, and then turned to protest politics full time. In

1966 he said, "We are a dangerous country, a neurotic country possessing deadly power." To get beyond the limits of American politics and change the attitudes of mainstream America required the devices of mass culture and mass entertainment. "Politics was just a circus," Rubin said, and protest should be entertaining and diverting. The manifesto that announced the birth of the Yippies in January 1968 struck that note. "Join us in Chicago in August for an international festival of youth music and theater," it proclaimed. "Rise up and abandon the creeping meatball."

During the first half of 1968 Rubin, Hoffman, and their associates gave the national press a diet of sensational threats and stunts that became the trademark of the Yippies. Jerry Rubin forecast that a pig would be nominated for president and then eaten, that the Democratic convention itself could be infiltrated and disrupted, and that mind-altering drugs could be placed in the Chicago water supply. The Yippies proposed "merely an attack of mental disobedience on an obediently insane society." Their fortunes and those of their leaders fluctuated with the tide of political events. When McCarthy and Robert Kennedy were attracting votes in the spring, the appeal of fringe protests faded. As the nomination of Humphrey seemed likely, the Yippies resolved to mount a protest in Chicago. At no time did they command any sort of mass following. But they succeeded in gaining a great deal of press coverage and alerting city and federal authorities to the prospect of erratic protest behavior.

The more conventional and political elements of the anti-war forces approached the Chicago convention at a low point in their fortunes. Johnson's withdrawal from the race, the start of negotiations with the North Vietnamese, the relative de-escalation of the fighting, and the candidacies of Kennedy and McCarthy—all these developments had drained some of the energies from the anti-war camp. And none of the major party candidates favored an intensification of the war effort in Vietnam. These developments produced disarray among the radical left. During the winter of 1968 they argued at length about whether to stage demonstrations in Chicago at all. Passions were also intense over the question of whether demonstrations should continue to be nonviolent. Should the anti-war forces look to violent action as a way of separating themselves from the liberal Democrats?

Johnson's withdrawal stalled decisions on a strategy for convention demonstrations. It also became clear that Mayor Richard Daley would use strong methods against protesters. Following the murder of Martin Luther King, Jr., Daley had issued a "shoot-to-kill" order about arsonists, and on April 27 Chicago police had broken up an anti-war rally with clubs and chemical sprays. The marchers, Daley said, were "hoodlums and communists."

After Robert Kennedy's death and McCarthy's faltering presidential campaign, the idea of a demonstration in Chicago revived. By the summer Tom Hayden, Rennie Davis, and David Dellinger were the most visible leaders in the planning for protests against the Democrats. Hayden was born in 1939 and educated at the University of Michigan. He had helped organize Students for a Democratic Society (SDS) and was the principal author of the "Port Huron Statement," which offered a critique of American society and a vision of what came to be called "participatory democracy." During the civil rights battles of the early 1960s and the anti-war protests that followed, Hayden became an articulate, celebrated radical personality. After a trip to North Vietnam in 1965, he came back convinced that the only goal for politics in 1968 was "to make it impossible for the next president to be elected without first agreeing to end the war."

Dellinger was an older member of the peace movement who had opposed American participation in World War II. His belief

that "all war is evil and useless" made him a conscientious objec-
tor and cost him three years in prison. Dellinger had marched for
civil rights and then turned naturally to opposition of the Vietnam War. In 1967, at fifty, he became chairman of the Mobilization to End the War, or "Mobe" as it was known.

Rennie Davis was born in 1940, attended Oberlin College,
and went into radical politics as a member of SDS. Hayden recalled that Davis "peered at you from behind thick glasses, with
a winning, almost excessive smile, his bright white teeth gleam-
ing even more than his blue eyes." Davis was the organizer of
the group who could turn Hayden's "raw visions into concrete
achievements."

The media often took the radical left at face value and de-
picted it as organized and cohesive. By August 1968 the reality was quite different. The events of the spring, including the
demonstrations at Columbia University, had produced factional splits and in some instances a willingness to use violence
to achieve goals. Tom Hayden believed it was "time to risk our
necks to take democracy back, a time no longer for visionary
platforms but for suffering and physical courage." At press conferences on June 29, Mobe leaders declared that demonstrations
were planned for Chicago, and in the event of violence "we will
physically protect our people and are already working on chemical deterrents."

Faced with what they saw as imminent threats to the convention and public order, Chicago authorities and the Johnson
administration prepared to protect the city from the anticipated
throngs of demonstrators. Having lobbied hard to persuade the
Democrats to meet in his city, Mayor Daley intended to take all
precautions necessary to ensure that disruptions did not mar the
occasion. Daley had been a major figure in Democratic politics
since delivering the state of Illinois for John Kennedy in 1960,
helping put him in the White House. Presiding over "the city

that works," he had been mayor for thirteen years. His roots
went deep into the city's Democratic machine, and his mastery of
the city faced no serious challenge. He and Lyndon Johnson co-
operated for their mutual benefit. When the issue of demonstrations came up at his press conferences, the mayor told reporters,
"No thousands will come to our city and take over our streets,
our city, and our Convention."

To block any confrontation, during the spring city and
federal authorities had been following the activities of radical
groups through surveillance, intelligence gathering, and secret
informants. The Federal Bureau of Investigation mobilized its
agents to weaken the left through a variety of tactics, including
anonymous letters criticizing its leaders, misinformation spread
to the press, and other acts of covert disruption.

When demonstration leaders asked for city permits to allow their protests during the convention and to sleep in the city's
parks, Chicago officials spent several months in lengthy negotiations before refusing to sanction rallies or marches. With the
prospects of a confrontation in the air if large numbers of protesters appeared, many on the left decided not to go to Chicago.
A few thousand showed up from around the country, and about
as many came from the immediate vicinity of the city.

Mayor Daley and the Johnson administration prepared for
the worst eventualities at Chicago. The police could put twelve
thousand men on the streets, and six thousand Illinois National
Guard troops were also assigned to duty for the convention. One
thousand Secret Service men were also in attendance. The FBI
added another group of its agents, and private security guards
were available as well. As a result, security at the convention
was extraordinary. Delegates had to present special identifica-
tion cards to gain entrance to the International Amphitheatre
where the proceedings were held. Around the convention hall
were fences and barbed wire. Outside the city were federal

troops ready to put down any evidence of civil disobedience and violence. The atmosphere of an armed camp foreshadowed the violence that would make the convention so damaging to the Democratic party.

Violence began as the convention opened. On August 26 police used teargas to force demonstrators out of Lincoln Park on the city's North Side, in observance of an 11 p.m. curfew. Officers pursued fleeing protesters as they ran from the park. The next night the scene was repeated. At an evening rally Jerry Rubin said, "If they try to keep us out of the park, then we'll go to the streets. They bring out the pigs to protect the pigs they nominate." After leaving Lincoln Park the protesters moved to Grant Park, near the city's Loop, where they stayed through the evening. On the afternoon of Wednesday, August 28, violence occurred at a rally in Grant Park that had been approved by city authorities. When a demonstrator appeared to be taking down a flag near the bandshell where the rally was being held, police moved in and clubbed some of those present. The crowd responded by throwing bricks, pieces of concrete, and food at the policemen. Shouts went up of "Death to the pigs" and "Fascist bastards." British reporters in the crowd later wrote that the police "went, quite literally, berserk."

Inside the convention hall the Democrats were tearing themselves apart. The crucial debate on the peace plank about Vietnam occurred that Wednesday afternoon. It was muted as both sides recognized that the outcome was a foregone conclusion. The anti-war forces did succeed in having the deliberations moved back to late afternoon, but that was their only victory of the day. The administration controlled the debate, arguing that a bombing halt would imperil the lives of American soldiers in the field. A Humphrey spokesman announced to the convention that "the Vice President fully supports the majority plank." The result was decisive in favor of the Johnson position, 1,567 votes in favor, 1,041 against. Peace advocates prayed and sang "We Shall Overcome." Others chanted, "Stop the war, stop the war!"

That evening the nominating process began. As it went forward, the most serious outbreak of rioting also erupted outside. It began at about eight o'clock and lasted for half an hour. Some three thousand Mobilization demonstrators and others were congregated near the Conrad Hilton Hotel on South Michigan Avenue. As the police attempted to prevent a march, many officers charged the crowd. A British correspondent recorded, "The kids screamed and were beaten to the ground by cops who had completely lost their cool." Some of the policemen chanted, "Kill, Kill." In the confrontation, spectators were driven through plateglass windows at the Hilton. During thirty minutes of violence the smell of teargas permeated the area, and the blood of those whom the police had beaten was everywhere. National television reporters had covered the event; their footage was prepared for broadcast later that evening. Foreign journalists, who had experience with the violent ways of police forces in their own countries, spoke later of the "ferocity" with which the Chicago police responded to events.

While the violence was happening, and as news of the events outside made its way into the convention hall, the ritual of nominating a presidential candidate had begun. Humphrey's name had been placed in nomination and a seconding speech was about to start when the networks were ready to air their coverage of the rioting. For almost twenty minutes the convention was forgotten and television viewers saw what had happened in the streets. The impact on the Democratic party was indelible. Here was abundant evidence that lawlessness seemed to accompany Democratic politicians and their policies.

The climax of the evening came when Senator Abraham Ribicoff of Connecticut, nominating George McGovern, denounced "Gestapo tactics on the streets of Chicago." The watching Mayor

Daley, sitting only a few feet from the podium, shouted a crude anti-Semitic remark to the senator. Ribicoff replied, "How hard it is to accept the truth." The rest of the balloting went forward later in the evening. Humphrey was nominated with 1,760¼ votes to 601 for McCarthy, 146½ for McGovern, and the remainder scattered among other candidates. When a television picture of Mrs. Humphrey was shown in the candidate's hotel suite, the vice president kissed the screen in happiness.

Humphrey had the nomination he had pursued for so long, but its value to him at the moment was dubious. The convention had left the Democrats torn into discordant factions and with an accurate popular perception that they could not keep their house in order. For Richard Nixon, watching in Key Biscayne, Florida, "it seemed as if the Democrats' convention was confirming every indictment of their leadership that I had made in my campaign speeches."

The events in the streets of Chicago produced two public reactions. In the minds of liberal Democrats and the radical antiwar elements, the actions of the Chicago police were convincing evidence of the bankruptcy of the American political system. As the police moved in, those fleeing them cried out, "The whole world is watching." The protesters seemed confident that the American public would sympathize with their treatment by Mayor Daley's cops. They soon found out how mistaken they were.

Polls taken soon after the convention showed that more than 71 percent of those surveyed supported the measures Daley had taken to maintain security. Fifty-six percent agreed with the way he had handled the disorders themselves. Defenders of the Chicago police emphasized the demonstrators' threats and provocations. "Those police took a lot of brutality from that mob, and they did their duty," said Senator Russell Long of Louisiana. The *Indianapolis News* concluded that "the demonstrators were in many cases openly violating the law, and in general seeking the trouble they got." Mayor Daley put out his own televised broadcast, offering his interpretation of what had happened. In the public relations battle in August 1968, the mayor of Chicago and his police force were the clear winners.

A federal investigating commission later decided that a "police riot" had occurred, a verdict that became accepted in the years that followed. The main figures among the organizers of the Chicago protest—Hayden, Rubin, Hoffman, Dellinger, Davis, and several others—were indicted on a charge of conspiracy to riot, and a celebrated trial of the "Chicago Seven" ended in convictions for some that an appeals court later overturned.

Hubert Humphrey recognized that the events in Chicago had been a "catastrophe" for his presidential aspirations. He had two opportunities to repair some of the damage to his candidacy before the convention adjourned. The choice of a vice president would indicate his priorities as a leader and his electoral strategy. And his acceptance speech gave him an opportunity to reach out to his defeated rivals and put some symbolic distance between himself and Lyndon Johnson.

Humphrey's choice for vice president was Senator Edmund Muskie of Maine. Muskie had attractive qualities. A Catholic of Polish background, he would offset some of the perceived appeal of Spiro Agnew to ethnic voters. Much quieter than the voluble and excitable Humphrey, Muskie seemed a solid contrast. Humphrey thought it was necessary to have "a competent able man who could do a good job as President" rather than "some kind of compromise for geography or ideology."

These were laudable sentiments, but Humphrey was acting as if he had already won the election rather than facing a campaign in which he was the clear underdog. It is hard to see what Muskie brought to the ticket in electoral terms. He helped carry his own state in the fall, but Maine's four electoral votes were scarcely crucial. Muskie's selection did not address those areas in which the Democrats were weak in 1968—the border states and the South, California, or west of the Mississippi River. The selection of a Southern governor such as Terry Sanford of North Carolina or Senator Fred Harris of Oklahoma would have been a sign that Humphrey was not conceding any section of the country to his opponent. Instead the Democratic ticket now had two Northern liberals from small states. The choice of Muskie won plaudits from editorial writers. It did not show Humphrey as a politician who was playing to win this crucial election.

Humphrey's aides urged him to use his acceptance speech as a dramatic gesture that would underscore his disagreement with Lyndon Johnson. They suggested that he resign as vice president and thereby declare his independence from the administration. When his advisers persuaded Larry O'Brien to put the idea before Humphrey on August 28, the candidate turned it down as "a gimmick." In a more telling appraisal of his continuing fear of Lyndon Johnson, he added, "And it will enrage the president."

Containing no surprises and no divergence from the policies of the Johnson presidency, the acceptance speech was a sound example of political oratory but not the game-changing moment that Humphrey's faltering campaign needed. He praised Johnson for having "accomplished more of the unfinished business of America than any of his modern predecessors." He promised that he would try "to bring a prompt end" to the war in Vietnam. He denounced crime because "neither mob violence nor police brutality have any place in America." Toward the end of the speech he called on McCarthy and McGovern for help "in the difficult campaign that lies ahead."

Having identified himself with the Johnson administration, Humphrey was not about to repudiate the president's policies. He offered no recognition of the sincere and legitimate protest movement that McCarthy and his followers had mounted. It might not have mattered. As he would during most of the fall campaign, McCarthy was staying aloof from Humphrey and his election. In a speech to his followers in Grant Park the afternoon following Humphrey's nomination, McCarthy referred to "the government of the people in exile." McCarthy's manner toward Humphrey was infuriating to the candidate, especially his refusal to appear on the podium when Humphrey accepted the nomination. Deferential toward Lyndon Johnson, Humphrey felt less sympathy toward the disaffected wing of the Democratic party.

Humphrey's public comments about the violence of the Chicago police added to the anger of liberal Democrats toward his candidacy. In a television interview, Humphrey said, "We ought to quit pretending that Mayor Daley did anything wrong. He didn't. . . ." When disturbances between protesters and police continued on Thursday, August 29, and into Friday, including a late-night raid against McCarthy's headquarters in the Conrad Hilton, the vice president was asked to intercede to stop the attacks. His press secretary declined to awaken him. The incident enraged McCarthy and helps explain his unwillingness to endorse Humphrey in the fall. In a 1971 interview, Humphrey said his experience with protesters during his campaign disposed him to think, "Well, they're just not decent people."

The Democrats left Chicago with their party in a shambles. The rioting in the streets had associated them in the minds of many Americans with lawlessness and disorder, precisely the charges that Richard Nixon and George Wallace leveled against them. Under the impact of the Vietnam War and the race issue, Democratic party machinery could not contain the deep divisions that had opened up during Lyndon Johnson's presidency. Among Democrats, resentments formed at Chicago persisted for years. While the rules changes that came out of the convention eliminated some of the inequities that had led to Humphrey's nomination, the unintended consequences of such reforms proved as disastrous as the earlier weaknesses they had sought to correct.

As the traditional Labor Day campaign opening neared in September 1968, the three contenders for the presidency began the race in very different conditions. Nixon was well rested and confident after a harmonious convention and a chance to court the various factions within his party. Wallace would not be nominated until mid-September when the American Independent party gathered in Dallas to make the obvious choice official. Polls indicated how well both Nixon and Wallace were doing. A Gallup survey after the Democratic convention showed that 43 percent of the electorate preferred Nixon, 30 percent was for Humphrey, and 19 percent for Wallace, with only 7 percent undecided. During the remainder of September, Humphrey's support fell away, and by late in the month Nixon opened a lead of 43 percent to 28 percent. Some Republicans began talking of a landslide victory.

Humphrey's campaign was feeble in every respect. Since he was trailing in the polls, his money dried up in a period before presidential candidates received federal matching funds. The vice president attempted to tap into some of the money that Lyndon Johnson had raised for the Democrats, but the president made it clear that neither he nor his fund-raisers would be at Humphrey's disposal. Despite the vigorous courting of Johnson in early September, the vice president could gain access to none of the president's money. He was forced to borrow money to fund his campaign advertising. Meanwhile disorganization characterized the Humphrey campaign. Lawrence O'Brien, Orville Freeman (the secretary of agriculture), Walter Mondale, and Fred Harris vied with other Humphrey insiders for control of the campaign. Worst of all, there was no overall blueprint for winning the election until a political consultant named Joe Napolitan hammered out a rough strategy in mid-September. He urged Humphrey to separate himself from Johnson on Vietnam and to point out his differences from Nixon on the issue of crime and justice. These were themes that might sustain a Humphrey rebound, but they were not yet in place while the campaign struggled during September.

Richard Nixon began his campaign with electoral assets that made his task much easier. During the 1950s and 1960s the Republicans created what became known as an electoral "lock." In that sense the 1964 election had been an aberration. Certain states were likely to be in the GOP column no matter whom the Democrats nominated. Nixon could count on at least 110 to 120 electoral votes from Indiana, Utah, Wyoming, Colorado, Oklahoma, Kansas, and other states that could not be wrested from him regardless of Democratic effort. Reflecting a shrewd appraisal of Republican chances for other electoral votes, the Nixon campaign selected fourteen states with 298 electoral votes as prime targets. Among these were California with 40 electoral votes, Illinois with 26 votes, Michigan with 21, and Texas with 25. Beyond that, Nixon hoped to contest Wallace in the border states of the South and a few Deep South bastions such as South Carolina.

The central point of the Republicans' advantage in 1968 was that it allowed them to choose their states of opportunity and use their extensive financial campaign resources with the greatest effect. Democrats, for their part, could count almost no states where victory was certain. Had George Wallace not been in the race as a third-party candidate, the Republican margin over Humphrey would have been decisive, since most of the Wallace vote either would have gone to Nixon or would have stayed home in November.

During September George Wallace's campaign seemed to be gathering momentum. He gained three percentage points in the public opinion polls and stood at 21 percent of the vote in a three-way contest as the month ended. His campaign style seemed as effective in the fall as it had been in the spring. He could reasonably expect to carry enough of the South to force the election into the House of Representatives. This electoral potential made Wallace an important element in the 1968 race, both for the issues he raised and for his effect on the major party candidates. The central theme of his campaign remained law and order. "Anarchists better have their day now," he told a California audience, "because after Nov. 5, you're through." He denounced the federal government for money spent to "trifle with my child's education." He pledged to return to the people "absolute control of public schools." On the issue of urban violence, he declared, "We're gonna have a police state for folks who burn the cities down. They aren't gonna burn any more cities."

To the dismay of Democratic leaders who were counting on a large union vote for Humphrey, Wallace seemed to be having a serious impact on labor support outside the South. As Humphrey recognized, Wallace was making an appeal in which "'crime' and 'black' got tied together, so that every threat" to the union members' "property or persons appeared to be a black threat." A United Auto Workers official in New Jersey summed up Wallace's allure for Northern union members: "The men in the plants want to zap the Negroes by voting for Wallace."

Wallace was scornful of both Democrats and Republicans. "If you can show me one thing the national Republican party has ever done for the average citizen of Texas or Alabama, I'll get out of the race for the Presidency because you can't show me one thing they've ever done." To one audience he proclaimed, "You get a bayonet in your back with the national Democrats and you get a bayonet in your back with the national Republicans." He charged that "the average American is sick and tired of all these over-educated, ivory-tower folks with pointed heads looking down their noses at us, and the left-wing liberal press writing editorials and guidelines."

For a moment Wallace seemed to be unstoppable. Hecklers plagued his rallies, but he used them as foils to whip his crowds to even greater enthusiasm and support. David Broder of the *Washington Post* observed that he had not seen a candidate "who communicates so clearly to his crowd, whose humor, whose warnings, whose admonitions and whose predictions draw the response that Wallace's do." Despite attacks on the Wallace sentiment as "an evil phenomenon" and the basis for a fascist movement, the former Alabama governor had the national political establishment scared.

The opening of Richard Nixon's campaign was also promising. With ample money to spend, especially compared with Humphrey's poverty, the candidate did not have to devote time to fund-raising. A professional organization managed Nixon's time to the best effect, and he appeared in staged events that showcased his abilities to the voters in the most attractive settings. Where Humphrey and Wallace had to deal with constant hecklers, Nixon's campaign excluded people who might disturb his rallies.

He began his campaign in Chicago, and the 400,000 people who turned out offered a striking contrast to what the Democrats had experienced just a week earlier. The crowds remained large and friendly during the weeks that followed. Nixon had worked out his standard campaign speech, which he delivered with practiced expertise. He brushed aside Humphrey's calls for a debate and pitched his appeal to the "Forgotten Americans, those who did not indulge in violence, those who did not break the law, those who pay their taxes and go to work, people who send their children to school, who go to their churches, people who are not haters, people who love their country."

On Vietnam, Nixon reiterated the position he had adopted since the beginning of the year. If the war continued on November 5, he told the crowds, "if after all the power and the support the Administration has had, then they've had their chance, now give us our chance. We will end the war on an honorable basis." For young people angry at the draft, he promised, once "our involvement in the Vietnam war is behind us," to "move toward an all-volunteer armed force."

His stance on civil rights was designed to position him between Humphrey and Wallace in a way that appealed to Southern voters. He endorsed the decision in *Brown v. Board of Education* but added that the federal government should not interfere with local school districts or use "the power of the Federal Treasury to withhold funds or give funds" in order to promote desegregation. He described efforts to transport children from slum areas to wealthier schools as futile. "They are two or three grades behind, and all you do is to destroy their ability to compete." When asked to appear in black districts, he declined. "I am not going to campaign for the black vote at the risk of alienating the suburban vote." His attitude toward black voters was stark. "If I am President, I am not going to owe anything to the black community."

The Nixon campaign presented its candidate to television viewers with a media skill that would be the trademark of Republican campaigns for the next four decades. Nixon was not comfortable in unscripted settings, and he did not project himself well on television, as his debates with John F. Kennedy in 1960 had showed. Given the proper context, however, Nixon could appear to good advantage. As one of his media advisers observed, "He should be presented in some kind of 'situation' rather than cold in a studio. The situation should look unstaged even if it is not."

His advisers used the format of Nixon as "the man in the arena" that had worked so well during the primary campaign. He performed in regional broadcasts which drew larger audiences than regular political shows. Campaign commercials struck the major themes of the Nixon candidacy. One showed a woman moving down a dark street while the announcer intoned, "Crimes of violence in the United States have almost doubled in recent years." Another featured scenes of urban rioting with Nixon saying, "We see cities enveloped in smoke and flame. We hear sirens in the night. As we see and hear these things, millions of Americans cry out in anguish. Did we come all the way for this?"

The combined efforts of the Nixon and Wallace campaigns put the Democrats on the defensive at the opening of the 1968 campaign. In the first weeks of September the Humphrey camp was suffused with an atmosphere of defeat. Yet by the end of the month the vice president's campaign had regained momentum, and the race tightened. President Johnson's diplomacy toward Vietnam also helped Humphrey throughout October. From the possible rout of the Democrats that seemed likely after the Chicago convention, the 1968 presidential election became a matter of suspense and surprises.

6

October Surprises

IN THE AFTERMATH of the Chicago convention, a revival of Hubert Humphrey's fortunes seemed highly improbable. Almost everything that could go wrong with a campaign did so as Humphrey struggled to find his message and connect with the voters.

Faced with an almost hopeless situation, Democrats decided to concentrate on their traditional base of support. They saw no possibility of carrying the South or most of the border states against either Wallace or Nixon. Because of President Johnson, they did not write off Texas. Humphrey hoped to run well in the Northeast and win California, Michigan, Illinois, and New Jersey. The aim of the Humphrey campaign was to emphasize that the choice lay between himself and Nixon, and in that way persuade liberal Democrats and moderate Republicans to choose him as the only sensible alternative to Nixon or Wallace. In a race among unattractive candidates that the historian Arthur Schlesinger, Jr., called "the battle of the minnows," Humphrey hoped to become the least-worst alternative.

First, Humphrey had to revive his own campaign, and that proved difficult during September. His initial rallies attracted disappointing crowds, and hecklers dogged him everywhere. As long as he was perceived as a loser, campaign funds barely trickled in. His managers had to go into debt to put television commercials on the air during the last weeks of the campaign. Democrats avoided him when he visited their states or cities.

Eugene McCarthy turned back all of Humphrey's pleas for assistance. Still angry over what had happened in Chicago, and seeing Humphrey as identified with Johnson's policies on the war, McCarthy kept himself aloof from the Democratic candidate. He traveled in Europe for a month, then covered the World Series for *Life* magazine. One of Humphrey's friends complained that McCarthy was "a slick political parasite—he always gives less than he receives and is mean as hell to boot." McCarthy's failure to endorse Humphrey, and his obvious disdain for his old friend, hurt the vice president among liberals.

Humphrey's overriding problem, however, remained Lyndon Johnson and the Vietnam War. No matter how Humphrey tried to put daylight between Johnson and himself, the president would not give him any. When his campaign opened in Philadelphia on September 9, Humphrey said he hoped to be able to remove some troops from Vietnam within a few months after the election. He also had kind words for the defeated minority plank at the Democratic convention. Misreading a newspaper story, Humphrey once again declared that American troops would be coming home—he failed to notice that it was only a routine replacement of one unit by another.

An irritated Johnson wasted little time in rebuking Humphrey. The Defense Department repudiated what Humphrey had announced. Even more wounding was the statement of the president himself. Speaking to the American Legion convention in New Orleans the following day, Johnson said, "We yearn for the day when our men can come home. No man can predict when that day will come, because we are there to bring an honorable, stable peace to Southeast Asia, and no less will justify the sacrifices that our men have died for." Humphrey would later ask himself, "I wonder why Johnson shot me down." Once again the president "made me look like a damned fool, and I never recovered from it."

Johnson's motives toward Humphrey during the first half of the campaign probably reflected his stroking by Nixon, so skillfully accomplished throughout 1968. The president also resented the efforts of people around Humphrey to separate their candidate from an unpopular president. Whenever Humphrey put one of his own people in a party leadership position, Johnson took it as a slight. Johnson told Clark Clifford he doubted whether "Humphrey had the ability to be President." He was disappointed that Humphrey had not "showed he had some balls."

Adding to Johnson's frustration were the gloomy prospects for his handpicked nominee for chief justice. In September, critics of the Abe Fortas nomination had complained about the money the justice received for teaching at American University during the summers. These Fortas opponents also questioned his role in advising President Johnson on policy matters and in speech writing. Support for the Fortas nomination had eroded. When the issue went to the Senate on September 25, Republicans launched a filibuster. Prospects for Fortas's confirmation seemed bleak once the minority leader, Everett Dirksen of Illinois, indicated that he would not vote for cloture to cut off the filibuster.

Defeat for Johnson came a few days later. On October 1 the Democratic leader, Mike Mansfield of Montana, tried to break the Republican filibuster. Needing two-thirds of the Senate to shut off the extended debate, the pro-Fortas senators could achieve a majority of only 45 to 43, far below the required number. The Fortas nomination was dead, as the justice and the president both recognized. Fortas asked that the nomination be withdrawn, and the choice of the next chief justice would be left to the winner of the presidential race.

By late September the men around Humphrey told him he must loosen his ties to Johnson on the Vietnam War. At one point he told a friend, "I think I've had Lyndon Johnson around my neck just long enough." But making a formal break proved difficult. A nationwide speech was scheduled for Monday, September 30, when Humphrey would be in Salt Lake City. His task was to distance himself from Johnson on the war without provoking a devastating response from the White House.

In the days that preceded the broadcast, tensions mounted within the Humphrey camp as advisers battled over the language of the speech. Polls showed Humphrey fifteen percentage points behind Nixon, and fund-raising was still slow. In speeches the Democratic candidate was subjected to intense heckling and booing. He could not go on as he had been doing throughout September. But how far should he move in separating himself from Johnson?

After many drafts and much squabbling about the content of the speech, the candidate hammered out an acceptable version almost at the last minute. He called Johnson and laid out what he would say. Johnson responded, "I gather you're not asking my advice." The language in the speech as delivered was cautious. "As President," Humphrey said, "I would stop the bombing of the North as an acceptable risk for peace because I believe it could lead to success in the negotiations and thereby shorten the war." He added that in making any decision he would take into account evidence of how the Communists would respond. "If the Government of North Vietnam were to show bad faith, I would reserve the right to resume the bombing."

One of Johnson's aides described Humphrey's statement as "fuzzy and ambiguous." So it was, but its tone was far more conciliatory to the anti-war wing of the Democrats than anything the administration had offered at the Chicago convention or during the weeks that followed. The public reaction was quite positive for Humphrey's campaign. His men told the press, "What he's really saying is that he'd pull the troops out and try to end the war January the twenty-first, 1969." Headlines indicated that he would stop the bombing, and signs appeared at Humphrey's rallies that said, "If You Mean It, We're with You."

Nixon issued a cool response to Humphrey's speech. "Humphrey either has to be for the bombing halt," said the Republican candidate, "or he has to support the negotiations in Paris." Nixon was unsure "which side he is on." In fact Nixon knew that the prospect of peace in Vietnam might undercut all his careful planning to achieve the presidency. He was aware that Johnson's announcement of an imminent peace would be "the one move that I thought could determine the outcome of the election."

The Nixon campaign had reached a high degree of optimism during the early weeks of September. With crowds so friendly, the campaign organization working smoothly, and the Humphrey campaign apparently collapsing because of its own inner problems, Nixon's aides thought for a time of such unlikely feats as carrying New York for the Republicans. A decisive victory for Nixon seemed certain.

Two areas of concern persisted. The vice-presidential candidate had proved more of a weakness than a strength for the ticket. Unskilled in national politics, Spiro Agnew had a flair for inept statements. He called Humphrey "soft on Communism," a phrase that revived memories of Senator Joseph R. McCarthy during the 1950s. Agnew referred to ethnic groups in demeaning terms. When asked why he did not travel through ghetto areas, he replied, "When you've seen one slum, you've seen them all." These comments did not hurt Agnew in the border states and the South, where Nixon was focusing his appeal, but they embarrassed Republicans in the Northeast. The Nixon campaign kept Agnew under closer supervision. Nixon rarely mentioned the name of his running mate.

The second problem was more serious. Despite Nixon's lengthening lead over Humphrey, most of his gain had come because the vice president had dropped in the polls. Nixon's own percentage of the vote remained at around 40 percent. One Republican analyst, Walter DeVries, noted this trend and worried that Nixon might not be able to push his numbers above the 40 percent range as long as Wallace remained a candidate. "This race is by no means in the bag for Nixon," he wrote. A Nixon aide and future columnist, William Safire, remembered that by early October "Humphrey was beginning to move up in our own private polls; organized labor was doing its job of winning back union members to the Democratic fold, and the erosion of the Wallace strength was going Humphrey's way and not ours."

Wallace's candidacy had slipped during the early days of October. The choice of a vice-presidential candidate hurt him. After considering several conservative figures, Wallace selected a retired air force general, Curtis E. LeMay. A veteran of the bombing campaigns against Germany and Japan during World War II, LeMay had led the Strategic Air Command during the 1950s and then served as air force chief of staff until he retired in 1965. He had suggested the United States tell North Vietnam "to draw in their horns and stop their aggression or we're going to bomb them back into the Stone Age."

The introduction of LeMay to the press on October 3 was a fiasco. The general defended the use of nuclear bombs and observed, "I don't believe the world will end if we explode a nuclear weapon." Wallace tried to soften the impact of LeMay's remarks, but the damage had been done. LeMay was also a poor speaker who added little to the Wallace campaign. Placards appeared at Wallace rallies protesting the vice-presidential choice: "Bombs Away with Curt LeMay." Within days of his announcement, LeMay was telling friends he was "fed up to his teeth" about getting into the presidential campaign.

Another problem for Wallace was organized labor's campaign against him. The AFL-CIO told its members in the North that Wallace had backed anti-labor legislation in Alabama. In addition, his state lacked adequate child-labor laws, had no minimum-wage provisions, and was stingy with welfare payments. Against these bread-and-butter considerations, Wallace's racial arguments lost ground in the North. Wives of union men did not follow their husbands into the Wallace column. As a result, the union vote returned to the Democrats in key Northern states.

Wallace soon slipped in the polls. His total fell from a high of 21 percent in late September to 13 percent by the end of October. The disorder at Wallace rallies, and physical attacks by his supporters against protesters, mocked the candidate's claims to be a champion of law and order. As the election neared, voters decided that either Nixon or Humphrey would soon be president and Wallace would not. One voter summed it up well: "Hell, a vote for him is wasted."

Wallace also confronted pressure from Republicans. Led by Strom Thurmond, GOP campaigners told Southerners that a vote for Wallace helped only "the unacceptable Hubert Humphrey." Spiro Agnew echoed this theme to Southern audiences. "Wallace is dangerous because he is not electable," he said in Charleston, South Carolina, in September. "He will divide the vote." For the most part, Nixon ignored the Alabama politician. On one of the few occasions when he referred to Wallace, Nixon admitted that he shared some of Wallace's frustration about "the rise in crime, the conduct of our foreign policy, what's happened to American respect around the world. . . . I'm against a lot of these things. . . . The difference is I'm for a lot things, and that's what we need now." In the last weeks of the campaign, Nixon made significant inroads in Wallace support in the South.

Both of the major party candidates adopted some of Wallace's law-and-order themes. Nixon stressed the issue from the opening of the campaign. In Dallas on October 11 he again promised "a new Attorney General who will launch an all-out battle against organized crime and guarantee the first civil right of every American—the right to be free from domestic violence." In a televised interview about urban riots, Humphrey assured viewers that "as President I would stop these outrages at whatever cost."

When Wallace stalled, the Nixon campaign felt the race tightening. To some degree the Republicans had overestimated their chances and had begun to act as if Nixon could not lose. They had an important advantage in their ability to dominate the media phase of the campaign. Republican commercials were better produced and well focused. Although the Republican candidate and his colleagues intensified their attacks on Humphrey as the campaign neared its end, Nixon followed his strategy of limited public appearances and controlled exposure to the press.

Republican overconfidence became a drawback. Nixon ran to protect his lead in the polls rather than to expand it. "We set out trying to save what we had, short of boredom," a party operative said after the election. When pressed, Nixon relied on the issue of law-and-order as the means of staving off the Humphrey assault. In Ohio he charged that Humphrey was "a do-nothing candidate on law and order" who had watched the United States "become a nation where 50 per cent of American women are frightened to walk within a mile of their homes at night." These themes, and the Republican advantage in electoral votes, were designed to keep Nixon ahead until election day.

Hubert Humphrey launched a final effort to save his candidacy and the Democrats during October. He did it in the face of formidable obstacles. Despite increased campaign contributions following his Salt Lake City speech, Democrats still lagged well behind Republicans in funds need to pay for television time. Humphrey challenged Nixon to debate him on national television. Remembering what had happened when he debated John F. Kennedy in 1960, Nixon was "determined not be lured into a confrontation, since Humphrey was still far behind me in the polls, and would be the beneficiary of any debate." Staging the debate would have required congressional action to modify existing equal-time regulations, and Republicans on Capitol Hill blocked legislation to that end. All Humphrey could do was denounce "Richard the Chicken-Hearted" and "Richard the Silent."

Humphrey's problems with Lyndon Johnson also persisted. The Salt Lake City speech had irritated the president. He told James Rowe, who had again asked him to campaign for Humphrey, "I'm not sure I'll do that; Nixon is more for my policies than Humphrey." By October 10 Johnson came around to a public endorsement of the Democratic ticket in a radio broadcast. The president denounced the "Nixon-Agnew record of reaction and recession" and urged support "for progressive Democratic leadership in America." Johnson also asked his wealthy friends to contribute to Humphrey's campaign.

Eugene McCarthy was not that forgiving. The Minnesota senator told New York Democrats on October 8 that he had run "to test the unity of the party on what we considered to be vital matters. I see no reason why if the cry for unity then was not acceptable, it is any more acceptable today." McCarthy argued that the Democrats should halt the bombing of North Vietnam unconditionally, accept free elections in South Vietnam, reform American draft laws, and reshape their party. Until these changes occurred, McCarthy said, he had no time for the Humphrey campaign.

On October 11 the political situation shifted in favor of Humphrey and the Democrats. Negotiations between the United States and North Vietnam in Paris, which had begun after Johnson's withdrawal statement of March 31, had been deadlocked.

The president insisted that any further halt in the bombing campaign in North Vietnam must have an acceptable response from Hanoi. Such an answer would include a willingness to have the South Vietnamese government participate in subsequent talks about peace. Until October 11 Hanoi had insisted on a complete end to the bombing of their country and opposed any South Vietnamese participation in peace negotiations. On that date, however, they indicated to the American representatives in Paris, Cyrus Vance and Averell Harriman, that upon a cessation of the bombing Hanoi would agree to accept South Vietnamese delegates to the talks.

Johnson and his aides knew that it was probably too late in his presidency to achieve an end to the war in Vietnam, but getting negotiations started would be a significant step toward a conclusion to the fighting. Any movement toward peace would also help Humphrey. To what extent, then, did Lyndon Johnson consider a peace initiative in October 1968 as a means of helping Humphrey and the Democrats win the White House? In part, the opportunity for such an initiative arose because, after Humphrey's Salt Lake City speech, the North Vietnamese probably concluded that the Democratic candidate was more likely to end the war than was Richard Nixon. So the chance to push for negotiations came to Johnson more because of what Humphrey had done than because of White House action.

Once the break in the diplomatic situation occurred, however, political considerations arose. During the extended deliberations that followed at the White House, Lyndon Johnson said, according to the notes preserved by an aide, "They think everybody is working toward electing Humphrey by doing this. This is not what motivates us." On the other hand, Johnson had told Humphrey in August that he would offer the vice president a better chance for peace than any speech Humphrey could make.

In Johnson's mind, his primary goal was the peace process, with Humphrey's election a happy by-product.

The Nixon camp feared the president's actions might snatch away an electoral victory that was all but won. On October 12 Richard Nixon received word from Henry Kissinger "that there was a strong possibility that the administration would move before October 23." A Harvard professor and adviser to Nelson Rockefeller, Kissinger had taken part in diplomatic negotiations about Vietnam for the Johnson administration in 1967. He had begun offering cautious advice to the Nixon camp in September 1968. At one point in late September or early October, Kissinger warned Nixon "about the moves Johnson may take." He predicted that Johnson "will take some action before the election." Nixon weighed Kissinger's words with great care.

For five days after the break in the talks at Paris, the White House sought to confirm various aspects of the proposed agreement with all the parties involved. The key point was the willingness of the South Vietnamese to come to the peace table before election day. Their situation was the exact opposite of their military enemies. Humphrey's September 30 statement seemed likely to make him less sympathetic to Saigon's view of the war once he became president. Nixon's election would give South Vietnam a president more favorable to its view. So President Thieu of South Vietnam had no incentive to agree to peace talks before election day. In effect, Saigon held an implicit veto over Johnson's peace plan. Thieu could not exercise it in public, but he was a clever man who knew how to use the machinery of his government for purposes of delay.

A lengthy series of meetings at the White House on October 14 produced new instructions to the Paris negotiators to go forward with talks aimed at a bombing halt and peace negotiations. They contained a significant new condition: Hanoi must open discussions within twenty-four hours after the bombing stopped. At one point, according to Johnson, his friends said, "The word is out that we are making an effort to throw the election to Humphrey." The next day both Hanoi and Saigon were delaying their response to the Johnson instructions. The condition of meeting within twenty-four hours was modified. It became a date to be set only after the bombing ceased.

On October 16 the president held a telephone conference call with all three presidential candidates to inform them of the status of the peace initiative. He told them he was requiring Hanoi to open talks after the bombing stopped and to limit hostilities against South Vietnam. That evening, at the dinner of the Alfred E. Smith Foundation in New York City, Johnson gently jabbed at Nixon in his "nonpartisan" remarks. "Pretty soon," he told the audience, "you won't have Lyndon Johnson to kick around any more." Privately he asked Nixon to "be careful" about what he had to say on Vietnam. The next day Nixon offered public support on a bombing halt because "We do not want to play politics with peace."

During the following week, rumors of an imminent deal with North Vietnam circulated internationally. In South Vietnam President Thieu pressed the United States not to allow representatives of the National Liberation Front (NLF), the Communists in South Vietnam, to take part in the peace talks. By October 21 Thieu was telling the American ambassador that the NLF should be at the Paris discussions only as part of the larger North Vietnamese delegation. Saigon's new demand was not likely to sit well with Hanoi. In the United States, meanwhile, Humphrey gained on Nixon as the election neared. By October 24 Nixon's lead had shrunk to eight percentage points, with 44 percent for the Republicans, 36 percent for Humphrey, and Wallace down to 15 percent.

With the election in the balance, behind-the-scenes politics became intense and dirty. Neither Lyndon Johnson nor Richard Nixon held back any of the weapons at his command. Nixon's careful planning and shrewd sense of partisan infighting gave him a decided edge. Through a Republican associate named Bryce Harlow, who had excellent contacts in the government, Nixon had a "double agent" in the Johnson White House. As Harlow later put it, "I knew about every meeting they held. I knew who attended the meetings. I knew what their next move was going to be."

In his memoirs, Nixon described Harlow's source as "someone in Johnson's innermost circle." That judgment was probably an exaggeration. Harlow's information could have been gleaned from a member of the clerical staff. In one case the agent said in error that White House aide Joseph Califano was attending the foreign policy meetings when in fact he was not. In any event, Harlow's information convinced Nixon that Johnson was seeking a bombing halt in order to aid Humphrey's election. Nixon became certain on October 24 when the source told Harlow that "an agreement had been reached with the North Vietnamese the day before."

The information was premature. No agreement with either North Vietnam or South Vietnam was yet in place. The president's urgency grew as the election neared. On October 25 the Soviet Union indicated it wanted a quick solution to the diplomatic deadlock. Since the White House attached great importance to Moscow's influence with Hanoi, the president hoped to move quickly but without attracting press interest. Johnson's efforts to keep the story under wraps fed the impression that the president was arranging a last-minute deal for Humphrey.

Nixon now moved to forestall the president. On Saturday, October 26, he issued a statement saying there had been "a flurry of meetings" to produce "an agreement on a bombing halt accompanied possibly by a cease-fire in the immediate future." He added that he had been told it was "a cynical last-minute attempt by President Johnson to salvage the candidacy of Mr. Humphrey. This I do not believe." Nixon was turning up the heat on the president.

At the same time the Republican candidate attacked the administration's defense policies. On October 24 he charged that "the present state of our defenses is much too close to the peril point," contributing to "a gravely serious security gap." Hubert Humphrey and the White House struck back at these statements. Johnson called Nixon's remarks "ugly and unfair charges," first about the nation's security position as well as "about our attempts to win peace in the world." Democrats suggested that the "Old Nixon," the politician of slashing attacks and partisan charges, had reappeared.

When he was a guest on the televised news program *Face the Nation* on Sunday, October 27, Nixon responded to the assaults on his Vietnam and national security statements. Supporting his attacks on defense policy, he cited Democratic senators who had warned of an alleged Soviet missile buildup. On the question of Vietnam he sought to align himself once again with Johnson's substantive position and to separate the president from Humphrey. "I back him up," Nixon said, "and I only wish that Hubert Humphrey would button up his lip and stick with the President on this." Nixon assailed "White House insiders" sympathetic to Humphrey who "were attempting to work out some sort of settlement."

At the same time he was supporting Johnson's negotiating position in public, Nixon was using another channel in an effort to stave off the bombing halt that might defeat his candidacy. Through Anna Chennault and the contacts established in the summer of 1968, the Nixon campaign encouraged the South

Vietnamese government not to yield to White House pressure. On October 23, for example, the South Vietnamese ambassador in Washington cabled Saigon: "Many Republican friends have contacted me and encouraged us to stand firm. They were alarmed by press reports to the effect that you had already softened your position." Another cable on August 29 reported that the ambassador was in touch with people around Nixon.

The National Security Agency intercepted these communications between Saigon and its Washington embassy as part of a constant monitoring of South Vietnamese diplomatic messages. Clark Clifford later described these activities as "extremely sensitive intelligence-gathering operations" in which the FBI and the Central Intelligence Agency took part. One key passage in an October cable from Washington said, "The longer the present situation continues, the more we are favored. . . ." With these facts in hand, Johnson directed the FBI to put Anna Chennault under surveillance, including wiretapping her telephone conversations. Nixon also believed that Johnson set in motion similar bugging and covert operations against the Nixon campaign plane.

The White House now had potentially explosive information about secret Republican negotiations with Saigon to block the peace process. The problem was that in revealing such information Johnson would also have to disclose *how* it had been obtained. What the White House had done was not illegal, but Mrs. Chennault was an American citizen who had identified herself with the Republicans. Surveillance might well be considered a partisan tactic. Moreover, disclosure of the Chennault-Saigon channel would reveal to South Vietnam that their codes had been broken. Also to be considered were Johnson's mixed feelings about Humphrey. Was defeating Nixon at all cost in the end what Johnson really wanted to accomplish? For whatever reasons, the president decided to press for peace talks without disclosing what the Republicans had done.

In the negotiations with Hanoi's representatives in Paris, October 27 proved to be another crucial date. North Vietnam proposed that the United States "stop the bombing on October 30" and agree that representatives from the National Liberation Front would be in Paris "as early as possible." This meant within three or four days after the bombing ended. At the White House, Secretary of State Dean Rusk said, "I smell Vodka and Caviar in it. We have substantial compliance. The Soviets have moved in."

Johnson now decided to order the American military commander in South Vietnam, General Creighton Abrams, back to Washington. In a series of questions he posed in the early morning of October 29, the president asked the general if a bombing halt was worth the military risk. Then came the decisive question: "If you were President, would you do it?" Abrams responded, "I have no reservations about doing it, even though I know it is stepping into a cesspool of comment. It is the proper thing to do."

Washington had made up its mind. What would Saigon do? Within hours the Johnson administration had the response. Thieu told the Americans he could not be ready by November 2 (three days before the election) because he needed to consult with leaders of his national assembly and members of his own security council. For two days the White House endeavored to obtain Thieu's formal pledge to come to the Paris talks. In one message Johnson said that Nixon had authorized the president to tell Thieu "that any messages reaching through any channel from Republican sources should be disregarded." The South Vietnamese president would not budge. Johnson concluded on October 30 that it was necessary to announce the bombing halt regardless. He had hoped to persuade Saigon to send representatives to Paris when the talks with North Vietnamese resumed on Wednesday, November 6, the day after the election. Johnson scheduled a national television address for 8 p.m. on Thursday, October 31.

Two hours before the program aired, Johnson placed another conference call to the presidential candidates to tell them what he intended to say. Richard Nixon felt "my anger and frustration welling up." Would his election be "undercut by the powers of an incumbent who had decided against seeking reelection?" In the broadcast itself Johnson used carefully phrased language. The Paris talks would take place on November 6, he announced, and the representatives of South Vietnam would be "free to participate in them."

The immediate reaction to the bombing halt favored Hubert Humphrey. By the time Johnson went on television, the presidential race had tightened greatly. Late polls showed Humphrey and Nixon only a few percentage points apart. The Lou Harris poll put the vice president ahead 43 to 40. Other signs pointed toward Humphrey. Eugene McCarthy had given him a grudging endorsement on October 29 as a man who has "a better understanding of the domestic needs and a strong will to act." Even Johnson had decided to throw his support behind Humphrey. In Texas the president had brought the feuding forces of Governor John Connally and Senator Ralph Yarborough into a temporary alliance. At a huge rally in the Astrodome in Houston on November 3, Johnson declared that Humphrey "should and must become the 37th President of the United States."

Last-minute Democratic optimism rested on fragile hopes. The electoral arithmetic still favored Nixon as the likely winner, and the Republican candidate had played his hand well on the issue of the bombing halt. Knowing that Thieu would refuse to send representatives to Paris, Nixon was not surprised when the South Vietnamese president announced on November 2 that his government "deeply regrets not being able to participate in the

exploratory talks." With that phrase the air went out of Johnson's peace initiative.

Nixon then used all his political skill to emphasize how the
White House had failed. He told television reporters that some
of his aides had concluded that Johnson had used the bombing halt for political purposes. But, said Nixon, "I do not make
such a charge." When Johnson called him to complain about the
Chennault maneuvers toward South Vietnam, he told the president "there was absolutely no truth in it, as far as he knew." As
Bryce Harlow recalled, "Probably Johnson didn't believe it. But
he probably couldn't prove it, I suppose." Nixon's link to Mrs.
Chennault was his campaign manager, John Mitchell, thus preserving the ability of the presidential candidate to deny knowl-
edge of her actions. During the last weekend before the election,
Nixon also had Mitchell instruct Mrs. Chennault to say nothing
further.

The full dimensions of the Republican involvement with
the South Vietnamese government in 1968 are still obscure. Intelligence information obtained by the Johnson administration
remains classified. Nixon's defenders accuse Lyndon Johnson of
using "dirty tricks" by wiretapping and electronic surveillance
of Mrs. Chennault and the Republican campaign. Democrats
charge that Nixon and the Republicans played politics with national security for electoral purposes.

In fact Richard Nixon did not have to persuade the Thieu
government to stay away from Johnson's peace proposal. It was
not in Saigon's interest to participate. But it is also clear that the
Republican candidate sanctioned communications between the
campaign and South Vietnam and thereby sought to counteract
Lyndon Johnson's efforts. If the information from the Chennault
channel had only a marginal impact on Thieu's decision, it was
not for lack of effort on the part of Nixon and his aides. When
they learned later of the White House surveillance that had oc-

curred in 1968, they thought themselves justified in adopting similar measures when they were in power. To that extent, the Chennault episode contained some of the seeds of the Watergate scandal of the early 1970s.

With the last-minute tide of opinion swinging back to Nixon, there remained one final card for Johnson or Humphrey to play. They could have broken the story about the ties between the Nixon campaign and Anna Chennault. The problem was just what Bryce Harlow had surmised: the only proof for the story lay in the intelligence information. Were it to be revealed, it would damage Johnson as much as it would hurt Nixon. Humphrey debated a long time whether to make the news public himself. He later recalled asking himself "if I should have blown the whistle on Anna Chennault and Nixon." Because he was not sure, and because such a charge would have been seen as an act of last-minute desperation, Humphrey said nothing about it to reporters. He later won praise for his decency; Nixon won the election.

Election Day, November 5, 1968, brought the long and troubled political process to a climax. The counting of returns stretched well into the early morning of November 6 before a definitive result was reached. Richard Nixon received 31,770,237 votes to 31,270,533 for Humphrey and 9,906,141 for George Wallace. That translated into 43.4 percent for Nixon, 42.7 percent for Humphrey, and 13.5 percent for Wallace. The outcome was more decisive in the electoral college. There Nixon won 32 states with 301 electoral votes, Humphrey carried 13 states and the District of Columbia with 191 electoral votes, and Wallace took five states with 46 electoral votes.

Nixon's electoral majority was a national one. He ran well in the West and Midwest, split the South and border states with Wallace, and carried four states in the Northeast. Because of Wallace's candidacy and Lyndon Johnson's efforts, Nixon lost

Texas, but he won other big states such as California, Illinois, New Jersey, Ohio, and Florida. Humphrey's strength was concentrated in the Northeast where he carried Pennsylvania, New York, and Massachusetts. His other large states were Texas and Michigan. He did not do well in the Midwest, where he carried two states, or the Far West, where he also won two states. The Democrats did best in the cities, among black voters, and with union members who resisted the Wallace appeal. Wallace's strength lay in his regional Southern base. He experienced the fate of other third-party candidates who falter when the voters concentrate on the major party hopefuls.

The closeness of the popular vote was deceptive. Four years earlier Lyndon Johnson had received more than 43 million votes against Barry Goldwater. Thus the Democratic total had dropped by nearly 12 million popular votes, a dramatic repudiation of the party in power. Nixon had increased Goldwater's total by more than 4 million votes, and Wallace had taken more than 9 million votes on his own. If the American electorate had cast its ballots for a liberal agenda in 1964, the result four years later suggested a conservative surge and a turning away from activist government.

In the wake of the elections, Democrats looked for reasons to explain their defeat. Party divisions received a large share of the blame. The impact of the national convention, the divisive primary campaigns of the spring, the reluctance of Eugene McCarthy to support Humphrey—all these were cited as reasons for Humphrey's loss. Others assigned Lyndon Johnson part of the responsibility because of his tepid backing of Humphrey and his insistence on adhering to his Vietnam policies for so long.

The two main issues in 1968 were race and the war in Vietnam, but they affected the outcome of the contest in very different ways. The prolonged war in Southeast Asia contributed in large measure to the disillusionment with Lyndon Johnson and his party that was so marked in 1968. While the American people had no desire to accept defeat in the war, neither did they wish to bear the cost of an elusive victory after the Tet offensive. As a result, all the candidates took a similar position in which they promised to bring about a satisfactory resolution of the war in a way that would minimize further American losses without humiliation.

The peace issue became significant in the final days of the campaign because of Johnson's proposal for a bombing halt and negotiations. The party and the candidate who seemed most likely to extricate the nation from Vietnam on reasonable terms attracted voter support. The swing to Humphrey upon the announcement of the bombing halt on October 31 gave him a chance to win an election he would otherwise have lost in a decisive manner. In the final crisis of his 1968 candidacy, Richard Nixon outmaneuvered Johnson and Humphrey in time to stave off the president's peace initiative.

The 1968 election was not a referendum on the war in Southeast Asia. The candidates blurred their differences over the conflict and found a common ground in promises to pursue negotiations and reduce the American presence in South Vietnam. In this aspect of the campaign Richard Nixon had a clear advantage. He lacked Humphrey's ties to the earlier policy of escalating the war, and he was not obliged to spell out a precise plan for ending the conflict. Although he never said he had a "secret plan" for bringing the war to a conclusion, Nixon fostered the impression that his foreign policy experience and contacts with world leaders would enable him to remove the United States from the war on more honorable and acceptable terms than Humphrey or Wallace could achieve. Only in the last days of the election, with Johnson's bombing halt, did Nixon's strategy on the war falter. The intransigence of South Vietnam restored the situation in his favor.

The major underlying issue in 1968 was race. It established the context in which the presidential election was played out. The defection of white Democratic voters—in the North to Republicans and in the South to Wallace and Nixon—shifted the political balance against Hubert Humphrey and his party. Richard Nixon and the Republicans were the direct beneficiaries of the wedge that race drove into the Democratic coalition after 1965. Republicans emphasized the legitimate concerns of white and black voters on the problem of crime. Nixon and his party also positioned themselves to assert his respect for the general principle of civil rights while retaining a reluctance to use federal power to compel desegregation in the South or to attack racial barriers in the North. The Republican position was a very palatable one to white Democrats who abandoned their traditional party allegiance during the mid-1960s.

George Wallace was an important contributor to this process. He provided white Democrats in the South with a reason to leave their party that had been so dominant in their region for decades. His argument that the federal government's racial policies were elitist offered a rationale for opposing Democratic liberalism that became a favored device of Republicans during the ensuing decades. As a result, Hubert Humphrey in 1968 won less than 10 percent of the vote among white Southerners. The traditionally secure Democratic base in the South vanished under Wallace's assault; after 1968 the Republicans inherited his support as the South became the most dependable area of the country for the Grand Old Party.

The election of 1968 thus left the Democrats weakened for a generation. With the South less hospitable to them, they had to run well in the rest of the country to win the electoral votes to elect a president. Because of the Republican strength in the Plains States and Far West, the Democrats had an almost impossible task to accomplish in winning the White House, as the elections of 1972, 1980, 1984, and 1988 demonstrated. Only in 1976, with the Southerner Jimmy Carter at the head of the ticket, did the Democrats capitalize on Republican division to win back the presidency.

The other chief liability for the Democrats after 1968 was their changed system for selecting presidential nominees. The reformed method of selecting delegates to the national convention, which was put in place after the election, gave considerable power to various interest groups within the party. Satisfying the diverse and quarrelsome Democratic constituencies resulted in weak nominees, including George McGovern in 1972, Walter Mondale in 1984, and Michael Dukakis in 1988. To avoid the excesses that had helped nominate Humphrey in 1968, the Democrats went too far in the other direction. Despite his flaws as a candidate, Humphrey was the strongest nominee the Democrats could have picked. Fairness in the process rather than the strength of the nominee became the Democratic watchword, at some cost to the party's chances in presidential races.

The advantage gained by Republicans in 1968 became a more enduring ascendancy during the twenty-four years that followed. Under Nixon, the GOP followed policies that attracted Southern whites in great numbers. The "Southern strategy" of grudging enforcement of civil rights undermined the Democrats as potential rivals in presidential races. Jimmy Carter slowed the process in 1976, but the failures of his administration confirmed the Republican advantage. In the 1980s Republican campaigns used the "wedge" issues of race, crime, and national defense to great effect to prevent Democrats from returning to the White House.

To avoid a potential alliance of white and black voters on economic issues, Republican strategy was to emphasize social and cultural questions that would split away whites with conservative views on race, crime, and moral values. An issue such as federal guidelines on busing worked in this way for Nixon in 1968 among Southern whites. Twenty years later Republican campaign chairman Lee Atwater used the issues of Massachusetts prison furloughs and the pledge of allegiance to the American flag to disrupt a possible electoral coalition between poor and middle-class Democrats for Michael Dukakis. Finding the right wedge issue became a standard tactic for Republican campaigns and represented an important legacy of Nixon's campaign in 1968.

The superior financial resources of the GOP in 1968 became another lasting Republican asset through the end of the century. The party built its fund-raising base among both large and small donors, and used these resources to hone campaign skills that the Democrats were slow to match. The party unity that Nixon achieved during his 1968 race became typical of Republican performances in presidential elections down to 1992. The result was a seasoned core of political operatives for Ronald Reagan and George H. W. Bush. As in 1968, the Democrats always seemed to be organizing their party in the midst of a campaign.

These developments fostered a sense of electoral entitlement among Republicans and the conviction that they were the natural governing party of the nation. They believed that Democrats were not a legitimate expression of the will of the American people. When Bill Clinton capitalized on the poor performance of George H. W. Bush as president to win the White House against the incumbent president and Ross Perot in 1992, Republicans treated him as a temporary usurper. The Republican recapture of both houses of Congress in 1994 brought divided government and a polarized politics that dominated the 1990s. In the process, the Grand Old Party lost the habit of governing and became intent instead on replaying the lessons of 1968 through subsequent elections to regain their accustomed majority status.

The triumph of George W. Bush in 2000, the winning of the Senate in 2002, and the reelection of Bush in 2004 renewed Republican aspirations for a permanent electoral majority. The legacy of 1968 still seemed strong. But the ground was shifting under the Republicans. The Democrats had won a plurality of the popular vote in the 1992 and 1996 presidential contests, and Al Gore had outpolled George Bush in the popular vote in 2000. In the congressional elections of 2006 the Democrats recaptured the House and the Senate as the Republicans found their base constricting. The presidential election of 2008 produced a victory for the Democrats behind Barack Obama, the first African American to be elected president. Gains in the House and Senate added to the Democratic advantage. Republicans found that the Southern core of their coalition was intact, but in the rest of the country the advantage they had first established in 1968 had evaporated.

As the first year of the Obama presidency demonstrated, the racial tensions of 1968 were still present. Republicans and conservatives questioned Obama's legitimacy to be president, and his critics on the right fell back on race to frame their attacks on the incumbent. Whether this strategy would result in a return to the Republican dominance of 1968–1992 would be up to the voters in 2010 and beyond.

Most of the primary actors in the 1968 contest had departed the political scene long before these trends became evident. Lyndon Johnson ended his public career on January 20, 1969, when Richard Nixon succeeded him as president. Johnson returned to Texas and died four years later in January 1973. Eugene McCarthy left the Senate when his term ended in 1970. He made several other runs for the presidency as an independent candidate but never reestablished the hold on liberal Democrats that made

him so formidable during the first half of 1968. McCarthy died
in 2005.

Hubert Humphrey was elected to the Senate to succeed Mc-
Carthy in 1970 and served there until his death in 1978. George
Wallace, elected governor of Alabama again in 1970, ran for
president again in 1972, but an assassin's bullet paralyzed him
during that campaign. He made a third run for the presidency in
1976, but Jimmy Carter defeated him in the South in the race for
the Democratic nomination. Having repudiated his segregationist views toward the end of his life, Wallace died in 1998. The
only major contender to emerge from the 1968 campaign with
brighter prospects than when he began was Ronald Reagan. Re-
elected governor of California in 1970, he lost a race for the Republican presidential nomination to Gerald Ford in 1976, then
won the White House in 1980. Elected to a second term in 1984,
Reagan returned to his California home in 1989 and died of Alz-
heimer's disease in 2004. Senator Edward M. Kennedy ran for
president against Carter in the 1980 Democratic primaries but
lost that race. He remained a major figure in the Senate until his
death in 2009.

As for Richard Nixon, the new president in his inaugural
address struck a note of conciliation: "In these difficult years,
America has suffered from a fever of word, from inflated rhetoric that promises more than it can deliver, from angry rhetoric
that fans discontents into hatreds; from bombastic rhetoric that
postures instead of persuading. We cannot learn from one another until we stop shouting at one another."

Unfortunately, Nixon did not make the theme of his inaugural the hallmark of his presidency. Instead of governing in the
national interest, he relied on continuous campaigning to ensure
his own reelection. His efforts for détente with the Soviet Union
and China, his Vietnamization of the war in Southeast Asia, and
even his approach to domestic policy reflected this overriding de-

sire to have a second term. In pursuit of that goal, Nixon condoned and participated in illegal acts as president that led to his resignation in August 1974 as a result of the Watergate scandals. He spent the last twenty years of his life seeking to rehabilitate his political reputation before his death in 1994.

The passions that shaped the violent and turbulent year of 1968, and so influenced the race for the White House, affected American politics for the next four decades. The Vietnam War ended during the 1970s, but its pain and division continued to plague the nation. The race issue remained a major element in national politics and a source of cultural discord even as the United States elected its first African-American president in 2008.

Writing about the election of 1968, the journalist Theodore H. White commented that "the marvel of American politics previously had been its ability to channel passion into a peaceful choice of directions." White's verdict was probably too charitable about earlier elections, but it caught something of the historical consequences of 1968. He suggested that "in 1968, hate burst out of the channel." American politics was changed for the worse in ways that the nation had yet to fully absorb or resolve more than forty years after Richard Nixon's narrow victory over Hubert Humphrey. Few elections have left a more enduring imprint on the direction of the United States than the contest that revealed the wounded soul of America in the 1960s.

Recommended Reading

Much of this book is based on original documents at the Lyndon Baines Johnson Library in Austin, Texas. This brief essay on published sources is designed to indicate where more information about the people and events discussed can be easily found.

Soon after the 1968 election, journalists published insightful accounts of the contest. Lewis Chester, Godfrey Hodgson, and Bruce Page, *An American Melodrama: The Presidential Campaign of 1968* (New York: Viking, 1969), by three British reporters, is thorough and well written. David English and the Staff of the London *Daily Express*, *Divided They Stand: The American Election 1968* (Englewood Cliffs, N.J.: Prentice-Hall, 1969), is a shorter narrative by another British team. Theodore H. White, *The Making of the President 1968* (New York: Atheneum, 1969), is the analysis of an excellent American reporter. Joe McGinnis, *The Selling of the President 1968* (New York: Trident Press, 1969), examines the Nixon media campaign.

Historical accounts of the year 1968 give most coverage to the Eugene McCarthy and Robert Kennedy campaigns. Charles Kaiser, *1968 in America* (New York: Weidenfeld & Nicolson, 1988), offers a cultural interpretation of the year. Other accounts include David Caute, *The Year of the Barricades: A Journey Through 1968* (New York: Harper & Row, 1988), and Irwin Unger and Debi Unger, *Turning Point: 1968* (New York: Scribner's, 1988). The best overall treatment of the election remains an unpublished dissertation by Dennis D. Wainstock, "The 1968 Presidential Campaign and Election" (Ph.D. dissertation, West Virginia University, 1984). Rick Perlstein, *Nixonland: The Rise of a President and the Fracturing of America* (New York: Scribner, 2008), is overlong and light on primary sources, but it offers a rich portrait of how the 1968 election fit into Nixon's political career. Walter LaFeber, *The Deadly*

Bet: LBJ, Vietnam, and the 1968 Election (Lanham, Md.: Rowman & Littlefield, 2005), is a synthesis of the election by a distinguished diplomatic historian.

The central participants in the election left memoirs of their campaign. Eugene J. McCarthy, *The Year of the People* (Garden City, N.Y.: Doubleday, 1969), reveals why McCarthy inspired so many people in 1968 and also why he lost. Hubert H. Humphrey, *The Education of a Public Man* (New York: Doubleday, 1976), has some fascinating chapters on the election. Richard Nixon, *RN: The Memoirs of Richard Nixon* (New York: Grosset & Dunlap, 1978), often says more than its author intended but requires careful use. Other helpful accounts include Anna Chennault, *The Education of Anna* (New York: Times Books, 1980); Clark Clifford, with Richard Holbrooke, *Counsel to the President: A Memoir* (New York: Random House, 1991); and Joseph A. Califano, Jr., *The Triumph and Tragedy of Lyndon Johnson* (New York: Simon and Schuster, 1991). Edward M. Kennedy, *True Compass: A Memoir* (New York: Twelve, Hachette Book Group, 2009), has some important insights about the Robert F. Kennedy campaign and Edward Kennedy's potential candidacy in 1968.

Among biographies, Arthur M. Schlesinger, Jr., *Robert Kennedy and His Times* (Boston: Houghton Mifflin, 1978), is thorough and favorable to its subject. Thurston Clarke, *The Last Campaign: Robert F. Kennedy and 82 Days That Inspired America* (New York: Henry Holt, 2008), is a favorable recounting of Kennedy's candidacy in 1968. George Rising, *Clean for Gene: Eugene McCarthy's 1968 Presidential Campaign* (Westport, Conn.: Praeger, 1997), looks back at the McCarthy insurgency. Dominic Sandbrook, *Eugene McCarthy: The Rise and Fall of Postwar American Liberalism* (New York: Alfred A. Knopf, 2004), considers the larger implications of McCarthy's career. Dan T. Carter, *The Politics of Rage: George Wallace, the Origins of the New Conservatism, and the Transformation of American Politics* (Baton Rouge, La.: Louisiana State University Press, 1996), is a perceptive treatment of Wallace's appeal. Herbert Parmet, *Richard Nixon and His America* (Boston: Little Brown, 1990), offers a sympathetic analysis of Nixon's role. Carl Solberg, *Hubert Humphrey: A Political Biography* (New York: W. W. Norton, 1984), treats Humphrey's campaign with thoroughness and insight. Robert Dallek, *Flawed Giant: Lyndon Johnson and His Times, 1961–1973* (New York: Oxford University Press, 1998), has much of value on the president's actions and motives during 1968.

On the important events of 1968, David Farber, *Chicago '68* (Chicago: University of Chicago Press, 1988), is very good on the crisis surrounding the Democratic convention. For accounts of the election from the perspective of the protesters, see James Miller, *"Democracy Is in the Streets": From Port Huron to the Siege of Chicago* (New York: Simon and Schuster, 1987), and Todd Gitlin, *The Sixties: Years of Hope, Days of Rage* (New York: Bantam Books, 1987). The domestic context of the race issue is explored in Thomas Byrne Edsall and Mary Edsall, *Chain Reaction: The Impact of Race, Rights, and Taxes on American Politics* (New York: W. W. Norton, 1991); Michael Flamm, *Law and Order: Street Crime, Civil Unrest, and the Crisis of Liberalism in the 1960s* (New York: Columbia University Press, 2005); and Robert Mason, *Richard Nixon and the Quest for a New Majority* (Chapel Hill, N.C.: University of North Carolina Press, 2004).

Index

A NOTE ON THE AUTHOR

Lewis L. Gould was born in New York City, studied at Brown University, and received M.A. and Ph.D. degrees from Yale University. He taught briefly at Yale before going to the University of Texas at Austin, where he is now emeritus professor of history. In addition to a great many articles and papers on presidential politics and Western history, Mr. Gould's books include *The Modern American Presidency*; *The Most Exclusive Club: A History of the Modern United States Senate*; *American First Ladies*; *Four Hats in the Ring: The 1912 Election and the Birth of Modern American Politics*; *Grand Old Party: A History of the Republicans*; and *Reform and Regulation: American Politics from Roosevelt to Wilson*. He lives in Austin, Texas.